The Hutterites

Lives and Images of a Communal People

Hofer Publishers

Copyright © 1998 Samuel Hofer
First Printing, 1998
Second Printing, 1999

Typesetting by Samuel Hofer, using Garamond typeface
Photo screening by Samuel Hofer
Book layout and design by Samuel Hofer
Cover design by Samuel Hofer
Text editing by Steven Michael Berzensky (Mick Burrs)
Copy editing and proofreading by Bernice Friesen
Additional proofreading by Monica Steffl
Printed in Canada

Photographs on front cover:
Top Left: Lehrerleit council member—photo by Lawrence Anderson, courtesy of Tony Waldner.
Top Right: Lehrerleit girls at Hutterite engagement party—photo from Samuel Hofer photo collection.
Bottom Left: Schmiedeleit woman baking buns—photo by Hannah Maendel, courtesy of Tony Waldner.
Bottom Right: Lehrerleit boys—photo from Samuel Hofer photo collection.
Photographs on back cover:
Left: Lehrerleit boys—photo by Lawrence Anderson, courtesy of Tony Waldner. Centre: Lehrerleit woman reading Bible—photo from City of Lethbridge Archives. Right: Lehrerleit girls—photo by Samuel Hofer.

Hofer Publishers
Box 9784
Saskatoon, Saskatchewan
S7K 7G5
CANADA
(306) 242-8162

Canada Cataloguing in Publication Data

Hofer, Samuel, 1962-

The Hutterites: lives and images of
a communal people

ISBN 0-9693056-9-9

1. Hutterite Brethren—History. I. Title.

BX8129.H8   H57 1998   289.7'3   C98-920081-7

In the memory of my grandparents,
Samuel and Suzie Wipf

Other Books by Samuel Hofer

Dance like a Poor Man *(1995)*
Born Hutterite *(1991)*

CONTENTS

Introduction

After reading about Hutterites in general, or after visiting a colony, outsiders sometimes get the impression this lifestyle is a utopia, believing that people in the colonies have few conflicts, aberrations, or problems. Others may feel that the highly structured lifestyle, well-defined roles, and boundaries of the community are too rigorous and constraining for individuals to lead happy and fulfilled lives. Neither viewpoint is true.

People do not always have peace. Life in the Hutterite colonies can sometimes be a hard road to follow. But it is not necessarily an unfulfilled life, plagued by tensions arising from narrowly defined roles in this close-knit religious society.

At its best, Hutterite life gives people a genuine sense of belonging and familial well-being. But most importantly—to a faith-filled Hutterite, at least—it offers a genuine peace in Jesus Christ. Although I am no longer of this faith, I acknowledge its strengths.

Throughout their 470-year history, Hutterites have experienced many struggles both within and without their communities. As you read about their way of life, you will gain a better understanding of the *Hutterisha Leit* (Hutterite people): who they are, what they stand for, and what their challenges are today.

In addition, I hope that the many photographs I have included, aside from providing a visual representation, help achieve a cumulative effect, giving you a broader perspective of Hutterite life than usually depicted.

Samuel Hofer
Saskatoon (1998)

Acknowledgements

In 1990, while writing *Born Hutterite*, my first collection of stories, I attended a reading at the Saskatoon Public Library. Andreas Schroeder read from his just-released book, *The Eleventh Commandment*, and showed slides from another new work, *The Mennonites: A Pictorial History of their Lives in Canada*. During his presentation, the idea came to me that I might someday publish a similar history about the Hutterites.

In the course of writing this book and searching for photographs, I talked with many people about Hutterite life and history. I am especially grateful for the assistance I received from the following individuals:

Tony Waldner, at Forest River Colony, North Dakota, whose love and dedication to Hutterite life and history proved inspiring; he also entrusted me with the photos in the Lawrence Anderson collection as well as with some of his own. **Leonard Gross**, consulting archivist, and his wife, **Irene**, who in 1993 welcomed me into their home while I did research at the Mennonite Historical Library and Archives in Goshen, Indiana. **Arnold Hofer** and his late wife, **Evelyn**, who invited me into their home whenever I passed through Freeman, South Dakota on my book promotion trips. Mr. Hofer's numerous translated works helped me appreciate the history of the Prairieleit Hutterites. **Mary Wipf**, for her hospitality whenever I traveled through Sioux Falls, as well as for her openness and directness concerning her Hutterite experiences. **Lesley Masuk**, in Lethbridge, for supplying me with research material and giving me much to think about. **Catherine Masuk** and **Edna Wurtz**, in Saskatoon, for their photos and comments about the Prairieleit. **Walter Hoover**, for his information about the Prairieleit at Langham.

I am also grateful to the following scholars whose work I leaned on heavily for some of the text material: **Victor Peters** *(All Things Common)*, **John A. Hostetler** *(Hutterite Life* and *Hutterite Society)*, and **John Hofer** *(The History of the Hutterites)*. There were many other books and articles that I referred to—these are all listed in the bibliography at the back.

This project would not have been complete without the practical editing help of **Steven Michael Berzensky**, also known as Mick Burrs. Mick was the first poet, writer, and editor I had ever met. Back in 1981, two years before I left the Hutterite community, I encountered this soul-filled poet at the Farmers Market in Regina, across from our colony table where we sold potatoes, corn, and cucumbers. Mick was selling Saskatchewan produce of another kind: poetry books and chapbooks. Little did I know that we would become friends years later, after I began publishing, and that he would agree to edit one of my books—this Hutterite history. (I believe there is no such thing as coincidence.)

Finally, I want to thank **Bernice Friesen** for her crucial help in the last stages. Even in the proofreading stage she helped me clear up some ambiguous passages and steered me further in the direction of objectivity.

TOP: Wolf Creek Colony, South Dakota, the site of the first Dariusleit Hutterite community in North America. (Photograph— LA/TW)

BOTTOM: Baildon Colony, near Moose Jaw, Saskatchewan. Established in 1967-68. (Photograph—SH)

TOP: Modern unit-houses at Rose Valley Colony, Saskatchewan. **Front yard and street.**
(Photograph, 1996—SH)
BOTTOM: Back yard and cow pasture at Rose Valley Colony, Saskatchewan. (Photograph, 1996—SH)

Hutterite Life

When traveling in rural areas of the Canadian Prairies and the American states of Montana, Washington, the Dakotas, and Minnesota, you will occasionally come upon small distinctive communities appearing as clusters of long buildings. These unique communities are often a short distance from a main highway or road, and usually no public roads pass through them. They aren't villages in the typical sense. Unlike Indian reserves where family houses are scattered, some separated by a few acres, these ordered communities are made up of several long unit-houses, a school and church, a large communal kitchen at the heart of the *huf* (community yard); laundry, abattoir, electrical building, waterworks building; shops, garages, numerous long barns, grain storage facilities, and other buildings. The residential area is usually at the center of the community and the farm facilities are located on the peripheral.

The people living in these communities, or colonies, belong to the largest, oldest, and most successful communal societies in the Western World. Named after Jakob Hutter, an Anabaptist leader during the Protestant Reformation in 16th century Austria and Moravia, Hutterites are one of four surviving Anabaptist groups—the others are the Mennonites, the Amish, and the Brethren in Christ. While these groups have similar beliefs, including adult believers' baptism and pacifism, the Hutterites differ primarily in their practice of communal ownership of property and communal living. In fact, they believe that salvation lies in communal living as practiced in the New Testament, Acts 2. Since their beginnings, their search for religious freedom and exemption from military service has taken them from Moravia to Hungary, Romania, the Ukraine, America, and Canada. Through their distinctive dress—black clothes, hats, suspenders and beards for the men, and polka-dot kerchiefs and ankle length gathered skirts for the women—the Hutterites are easily recognized when they come to towns and cities in the areas where they live.

Hutterite society is different from mainstream North American society in obvious ways. The close-knit cultural and religious communities follow unique traditions and dress in fashions that appear outlandish to outsiders. However, look past the appearance and you discover that their cultural and religious affiliations are not that much different from western orthodox traditions after all. Furthermore, meet individuals from these communities and you find they are hardly mysterious people as many people think. What makes the Hutterites so striking in North America, in spite of their own modern communities, are their appearance and customs reminiscent of centuries long past. But their lifestyle and religion should not be considered merely the eccentricities of a folk group that has not yet caught up with the times. Many millions of people fully integrated into the modern world believe literally in the ancient teachings of the Bible and order their lives accordingly. Hutterites are no different.

The Leit

Hutterites have three distinct subgroups. Each group, although their belief systems are more or less the same, is like a separate denomination, with its own discipline, and they don't usually intermarry. The names of these groups are *Schmiedeleit, Dariusleit,* and *Lehrerleit.* The word "leit" means folk, or people. All originate from the three founding colonies that migrated from the Ukraine to South Dakota between 1874 and 1879. The Schmiedeleit (Blacksmith People) were named after their leader Michael Waldner, who was a blacksmith and preacher. The Dariusleit were named after their preacher, Darius Walter. The

David Hofer, one of the council brethren (Lehrerleit) at Springside Colony, Alberta. Mr. Hofer died in 1998. (Photograph—LA /TW)

Lehrerleit (Teacher's People) were named after Jakob Wipf, who was a teacher and preacher. Today, the Schmiedeleit are located in Manitoba, the Dakotas, and Minnesota. The Dariusleit and Lehrerleit live interspersed in Saskatchewan, Alberta, and the states of Montana, and Washington. At the time of this writing (1998) there are nearly 40,000 Hutterites living in 408 colonies, and about twenty new communities are being established.

There is a fourth Leit, once commonly known as the *Prairieleit* (People of the Prairie). These are descendants of Hutterites who didn't favor communal living upon settling in America, but chose to settle on homesteads instead, establishing individualistic Hutterite churches, then eventually assimilating into adjoining Mennonite and other communities. They can aptly be considered "a neglected people," because scholars have regretfully overlooked their significant history, despite their representing about two-thirds of the entire Hutterite population that emigrated from Russia. I have included a chapter about these non-communal Hutterites in this book. I feel their history—at least in how it relates to the communal Hutterites—deserves more than just a brief mention, as most authors writing about the Hutterites have done in the past.

All people living in the world outside the Hutterite communities are called *die Welt Leit* (the People of the World). Another term that is commonly used for people outside the colony is *die Englisha Leit* (the English People), because they are from the English-speaking world. Because the Hutterites' first language is German, they consider themselves from the German-speaking world, in their case, from the *Gmanshofter* (Community people).

The Integrated Community

When a Hutterite colony has *gman urnung* (community order), it is esteemed spiritually successful. The community's structure, or rather, its hierarchy, is thought to be divinely ordained, giving older people authority over younger people, men authority over women, and the community authority over the individual. In a spiritual sense, the community is looked upon as Mother, the caregiver. God, who ultimately has authority over the community, is looked upon as Father. The colony is also often referred to as the "ark." A person leading a Christian life in the colony is considered to be in the ark. Those living outside aren't considered to be fully under this covenant.

Each of the three Leit has a senior elder, known as the *vorsteher* (bishop). His role is to provide spiritual leadership for the entire Hutterite fellowship in his group. At the head of each colony is the preacher, the spiritual leader, who is nominated by the brethren (baptized men only) and preachers from other colonies. The nominees' names are written on separate pieces of paper, placed in a hat, and drawn by lot, leaving the final decision up to providence. The minister receives no formal training for his position. All colonies also elect an assistant preacher who, after a colony branches out, becomes the head preacher of the new colony. After a trial period of a year or more, during which time he grows into his leadership role, he is ordained by the bishop to the office of head minister. Working closely with the financial manager, he also assumes the role of president and secular leader, which involves every aspect of colony life. He acts as mediator in disputes (not always successfully), administers punishment, disseminates information, interprets doctrines, and otherwise acts as "shepherd of the flock." In a small community, where most people are related, this position can be most challenging. A minister prone to taking sides in family disputes, and who doesn't possess a good deal of tact, fairness, and skill when dealing with people, often leaves a long trail of disorder and distrust. When there is *urnung*, there is usually an honest and very capable preacher in charge, whom people respect.

At the head of the brethren is a council, usually consisting of five or six men, who are elected and hold key positions in the administration of the colony. Among these are the preachers, financial manager, field manager, and other elders. Often the German teacher also serves on this council. His job is a rather exalted occupation, commanding a lot of respect. He is, in

Lehrerleit woman reading Bible. (Photograph, 1976—CLA)

fact, a minister in his own right, because he indoctrinates the youth in the Hutterite religion through the teaching of Bible stories, Hutterite history and language. He is also the primary disciplinarian of the school children outside the family unit.

People are expected to respect the decisions made by the council brethren. The actions of this council are in turn directed by the whole congregation of baptized men. The steward has the responsibility of financial management of the colony. Although he makes daily financial decisions, when major purchases are made (machinery, land, buildings, and so on), the brethren determine the outcome by a discussion, followed by a vote. That said, however, the influence of young people has increased dramatically over the years. Although elders remain the primary decision-makers, changes are most often suggested by the younger generations.

The labor force in the colony is also structured, in part, according to age and gender. Mostly, men do the farm work: livestock, grain farming, manufacturing, etc. The women do most of the domestic work, such as cooking, baking, canning, and gardening. The overseer of the garden (always a man) is generally either the German schoolteacher (also always a man) or one of the preachers. The brethren elect men to positions such as cattleman, hogman, chickenman, carpenter, blacksmith, plumber, and truckman. The other men, including teenagers already finished with school, are assigned to help any of the men in the above positions, and to operate equipment on the fields. Quite often, particularly when a community's population is small, some men will hold more than one position. To maintain a colony's effective and organizational unit, a daughter colony is established at a new location when a colony's population reaches 125 or more and there isn't sufficient work for everybody. Approximately half the population then moves to the new location. An average colony has about ninety people, or about fifteen families.

There are also supervisors among the women, including the head cook, the head seamstress, the garden woman (usually the garden overseer's wife), and the two to three kindergarten teachers who rotate days. Traditionally, the

women, ranging in age from seventeen to forty-five, take turns, in pairs, working one week in the bakery, then another week in the kitchen, under the supervision of the head cook. Every day three meals are served in the communal dining hall, situated in the center of the colony yard. Men sit on one side of the hall and women on the other, according to age. A bell situated on top of or beside the long communal kitchen calls people to the hall. The members of "die Leit" (people older than fourteen or fifteen) eat separately from the children. The colony's two preachers also eat separately, in the head preacher's home. This privacy gives them a chance to discuss both spiritual and non-clerical issues on a daily basis, serving also to apprentice the second preacher for the time when he too will lead a colony. In some communities, women have reorganized their traditional cooking duties. This is done to offer more convenience to individuals, since some women prefer to cook for several weeks at a stretch and then be free for the rest of the time, enabling them to visit other colonies for longer periods.

Sometimes people outside the Hutterite community point out that this patriarchal society isn't fair to women. Women don't vote; in most colonies they don't drive; and in church as well as at the communal dining table, men and women are segregated. Roles are quite narrowly defined. True, in comparison to women's roles in mainstream society, it is not fair. Hutterite religion is based on literal interpretation of the Bible, which says the man should be the head of the house, the woman must wear a head covering, the wife should submit to the husband, and so on. I doubt Hutterite women are always happy with this official arrangement, but it appears they are reasonably comfortable and secure in their roles. When asked, most women say they don't mind it: "We do our work, the men do theirs." To me, this answer is less than satisfactory, but it clearly shows how much biblical influences are still part of Hutterites' collective psyche.

Nevertheless, Hutterite women do contribute their female-oriented perspective into how a colony is run, if indirectly. Men never go to a meeting without input from their wives, sisters, or mothers whenever issues that will affect the women are to be discussed. The women always contribute to the consensus that precedes voting. This indirect power is evident in the Hutterite saying: "The man is the head of the house, the woman is the neck that turns the head." Hutterite women are very vocal and the impression that their men dominate them is for the most part, wrong. In family situations, couples work closely as partners. Each fulfills his or her role as ordered by the community and traditions.

TOP: Hutterite woman's rolling pin. (Photograph—LA/TW) .
BOTTOM: Woman ringing bell at community kitchen and dining hall at Milford Colony in southern Alberta. Milford Colony is one of the oldest Lehrerleit Hutterite colonies in Canada (1918). In the 1970s, the Hutterites stopped building houses in the traditional style. High gable roofs and attics that extended over all the family units were no longer fashionable when indoor toilets and modern apartments with basements became more popular. Some colonies kept the original structures, remodeling the insides only. See Baildon Colony on page 13. Most colonies dismantled the old buildings and built new ones. (Photograph, 1976—CLA)

Broom making, a good job for a semi-retired Hutterite man. (Photograph—LA/TW)

TOP LEFT: Schmiedeleit woman baking buns at Forest River Colony, North Dakota. (Photograph, 1980s—HM/TW) **TOP RIGHT: Lehrerleit men at Ponderosa Colony, Alberta, planting a 1,400-foot windbreak of caragana trees to protect their garden.** (Photograph, 1976—CLA) **BOTTOM: Lehrerleit baby sitters at Rose Valley Colony, Saskatchewan, pushing traditional Hutterite children's wagons.** (Photograph, 1997—SH)

**TOP: Poultry manager, Joseph
Maendel, at Forest River Colony, North
Dakota.** (Photograph, about 1970—TW)
**LEFT: Ducks at Glendale Colony,
Montana.** (Photograph—SH)
RIGHT: Lehrerleit girls washing floor.
(Photograph, 1970s—LA/TW)

Lehrerleit boys. (Photograph—LA/TW)

Schools and Vocations

Hutterite children attend kindergarten from two-and-a-half or three years of age until their fifth or sixth birthday. At this early age, training for Christian communal living begins. Aside from universal lessons such as sharing, cooperation, and respect for others, Hutterites believe that children must have their "self-will" broken early and their psyche infused with a spiritual outlook crucial for a life dedicated to communal living. Generally, two or three older women in the community are assigned to the position of *klana schul ankela* (kindergarten mothers), who serve on a rotational basis. These women teach the children traditional German songs and prayers by rote. No drawing, writing, or reading is taught. At this stage all the teaching is oral. Corporal punishment (two or three slaps on the palms with a leather strap) is still sanctioned by most Hutterite colonies. There is plenty of time for playing, both in school and out, but to Hutterites, school is not solely a place of secular activity and training—it is also designed to indoctrinate children with traditional beliefs. For the most part, higher education is considered unnecessary for the Hutterite way of life.

At age six or seven, the children start Grade 1 in English school, following the same curriculum as most public schools, and continue through to Grade 8 or 9, or until age fifteen, whichever comes first. Simultaneously, they attend German school. Some students may even complete Grade 10, taking correspondence classes. While this amount of formal education is not nearly enough outside the community, it does seem to suffice for Hutterite life. English school is taught by a certified non-Hutterite teacher. A teacher new to Hutterite life and ways often finds this job very challenging. Much patience and skill is required. Someone with problems of his or her own and lacking a dynamic personality has a tough time teaching in a Hutterite community. While colony life itself may seem idyllic, a non-Hutterite soon realizes that teaching youngsters who at first know little or no English is not an easy task. At age six or seven, the students are suddenly thrust into English school, often with a teacher who knows no German. It can be an instant culture shock for both pupils and instructor. Furthermore, a teacher must be sensitive to the religion and traditions of the Hutterites. Sex education and teaching about evolution are taboo. Sex education is left to the parents. One English school teacher who works in a colony near Biggar, Saskatchewan, told me she had gotten "tuned in" by the colony's German school teacher for suggesting to the boys that they could help the girls with the sweeping and cleaning up. Apparently, the German teacher felt that the English instructor had overstepped the traditional boundaries. In the past, teachers in colonies were often desperate for courses that would simplify the logistics of instruction in a multilevel classroom—grading, marking, and assessing pupils' progress. The turnover for secular teachers was quite high. Since then, beginning in the 1980s, administrators of school systems have made strides in tailoring course materials for Hutterite classrooms, making it easier for teachers to work efficiently. If a teacher is able to continue until he or she feels at ease with the cultural differences, teaching becomes very rewarding and more relaxing than in public schools. All English schoolteachers I have talked to have told me that most Hutterite students love learning and are voracious readers. Without the distractions of TV, radio, and the outside world in general, the students are very focused on their studies. One teacher said he uses newspaper stories—which aren't prohibited—to teach current events. "The colony won't allow me to bring audio-visual aids into my class," he said. "It would be very easy for the kids to think the world as just one succession of Hutterite colonies."

With the exception of busy summer months, children attend German school for an hour in the morning (before regular English school), and another hour or more late in the afternoon. With these two extra hours five days a week, another two hours on Saturday, an hour of Sunday school, and worship services on a daily basis, a Hutterite child's week is quite full. English is more or less the language used for secular learning and German for religious and moral training. There is no grading in German school. The German teacher is always a member of the colony. In German school, reading, writing,

TOP: Lehrerleit
kindergarten. (Photograph,
1980s—LG)
BOTTOM: Lehrerleit English
school students. (Photograph,
1980s—NM)

grammar, and handwriting skills are taught. The materials used for instruction are stories with strong moral messages, biblical scriptures, and Hutterite martyr ballads and other hymns dating back to the 16th and 17th centuries, when Hutterites were prolific in the writing of songs and sermons. In most colonies (more universally, the Lehrerleit), the students memorize songs, certain scriptures, and a condensed version of the Old and New Testament for recital in morning German school. The number of verses memorized varies. It depends on a group's ability. Toward the end of my school years, at age fifteen, my classmates and I sometimes recited as many as fifteen 8-line verses of songs that we had already memorized once or twice. Of new material, we memorized four to six verses. When going over previously learned verses, we took turns until all the verses were recited, which meant that each of us recited only four or five of the fifteen. However, since nobody knew who would start the first verse, we had to memorize them all.

Memorizing verses and scriptures is also a common Sunday school activity. At Easter and Christmas, young people are required to recite numerous songs. I still have dreams of being stuck in Sunday school, not able to recite my verses. This usually happens when I am procrastinating at something. My subconscious mind takes me back to my young adult years. Regardless of how hard I try, the words simply escape me. The dreams are always the same and I always find some excuse for not going to school. In the end, guilt overtakes me and I decide to leave the colony. Just as I am leaving, I awaken, relieved to remember that I left many years ago.

In recent years some Schmiedeleit colonies, particularly in Manitoba, have begun looking to their own members to teach the public school curriculum. In this area, the Schmiedeleit are more progressive than the more conservative Lehrerleit and Dariusleit. Through the leadership of former Schmiedeleit bishop (Jacob Kleinsasser) and colony educators, this group has made changes in how academic education is perceived in the colonies. In 1994, twenty-one Hutterites entered a newly developed Hutterite Education Program at the University of Brandon. The program has about the same number of men and women. In 1998, the first group graduated, and

are now teaching the public school curriculum in their colonies. Incidentally, at least two Hutterite instructors who have been teaching the public school curriculum for a few years are women. Anna and Dora Maendel at colonies near Portage La Prairie have been instrumental in leading the way to higher education for their people. But even among the Schmiedeleit, some people are concerned about sending young Hutterites off to college. In the early days in America, the colonies did send a dozen married men to college for this same reason. Some did not come back. Apparently, this was too high a cost and the practice was discontinued.

According to an article published in the *Winnipeg Free Press*, between 1991 and 1996 the number of Hutterites taking high school courses though telephone links to a centrally located teacher jumped from eighteen to 717! To the dismay of conservative Hutterites, by the end of 1997, two Manitoba colony schools had even published their own web page on the Internet. A typical response from the more conservative groups, Lehrerleit and Dariusleit, is that the Manitoba colonies are too loose. "They (Schmiedeleit) may want it," they say, "but they have problems." The critics are referring to the problems the Schmiedeleit have experienced since 1989, causing a schism in the Hutterite church. I have included this history in the chapter titled "When East Met West."

This emphasis on higher education will without doubt create even more distance between the colonies than already exists. The Hutterite communities in the next century will see a continuation in the trend for increased diversity. As land prices rise and their economies and communities become increasingly complex, it is inevitable that more and more colonies will be looking to other industries besides farming. It will be interesting to see how this will effect them individually and collectively. Incidentally, in the State of Washington, the Dariusleit appear to be more liberal minded than the average Dariusleit in Sakatchewan and Alberta, allowing their students to complete High School.

Generally, Hutterite children learn the skills of adulthood from their parents and older relations around them. Young girls are taught babysitting skills, taking care of younger siblings or other families' children whenever the mother is away from the house. The girls also perform various domestic duties in the community. After age fifteen, they learn skills such as sewing, cooking, slaughtering poultry or other livestock, gardening and domestic tasks, most of which are done as part of a crew. The boys also learn by doing. By age fifteen, they have acquired a few basic skills, such as driving tractors and working with basic tools and with livestock. At that age, with their school years behind them, the boys begin moving through all the operations of the colony, apprenticing under older members. While their formal education may stop at age fifteen, boys' vocational training continues into adulthood. Generations of equipment operators, mechanics, plumbers, woodworkers, metalworkers, and electricians pass their skills on to later generations.

In a fast changing technological world, Hutterites are also required to learn new skills. The dairyman at a colony in southern Saskatchewan said that after his colony computerized its dairy system, he locked himself in his office for three months while he taught himself how to use the computer. "It was hard to begin with and I was starting to wonder if I'd ever grasp it all," he said. "But then, one day, like a roadmap, it all unfolded, and I haven't looked back since."

Each cow in this dairyman's herd now wears a high-tech necklace around her neck, which is a sensing mechanism connecting the cow to a main-frame computer. When the cow enters the feeding chute, the computer registers the amount of feed she has consumed in a twelve-hour period. The dairyman can get a read-out on any cow in his herd. The computer allows a certain amount of feed to come from the feeding chute. Once the cow has consumed her allotted rations, no more feed will be dispensed. If she doesn't eat her rations, the dairyman is quick to check for possible illness. "This takes the guess-work out of my job," he said, "because we are able to feed individual cows exactly what they require. This does away with the shotgun feeding approach that is used by many producers out there."

Unlike their Amish cousins, Hutterites use the most modern equipment available for large-scale agricultural operations (6000-15,000 acres), which include poultry and livestock farming. Their view on technology is simply this: *It is not the thing itself that is good or bad, but the use to which it is put.* As long as the communal system is maintained, each colony is free to adopt the solution that suits its economic needs. The welfare of the community is the first priority. In all practicality, if new technology can make work easier and increase efficiency, there is no reason not to adopt it. Hutterites are a proud people and place much value on order, organization, and good enterprise. They are astute business administrators, and today their colonies are relatively wealthy. At an individual level, all members are part of an intensely communistic society, while the community on the whole operates in a very capitalistic manner.

TOP: Modern school at Rose Valley Colony, Saskatchewan. (Photograph, 1998—SH)
BOTTOM: German school teacher and students at Forest River Colony, North Dakota. (Photograph—TW)

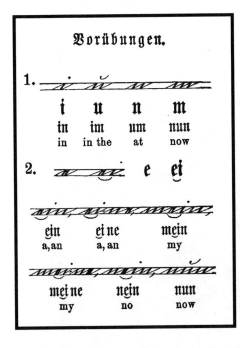

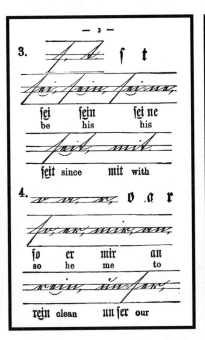

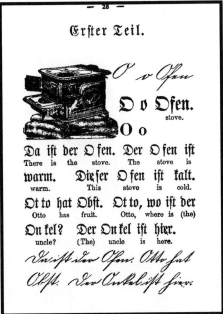

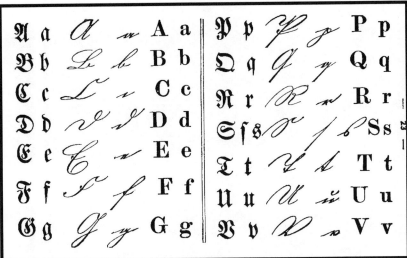

Sample pages of the *Herald German English Primer,* used in Hutterite German schools since 1926. Note the old German hand script, which the Hutterites have preserved. In German school, students hand-copy several volumes of traditional songs and Bible verses, using them for memorization and recital. After finishing German school at age fifteen, graduates continue using the books in Sunday school for the same purpose. Traditionally, the Hutterite sermons were also written in this style.
Reprinted from the German English Primer, Edwards Brothers, Inc.

Dariusleit mother and daughter cleaning sunflower seeds in the wind at Riverview Colony, Saskatchewan. (Photograph, 1982—Rolf Brednich)

TOP: Lehrerleit blacksmith working with a lathe. (Photograph, 1970s—CLA)
BOTTOM: Schmiedeleit plucking slaughtered geese. (Photograph, 1979—HM/TW)

31

Hutterites at Miller Colony, Montana, butchering hogs. Every fall, each colony butchers several large pigs for consumption over the winter. The meat and various parts of the pigs provide smoked hams, bacon, several types of sausages, pork-filled perogies, headcheese, lard, and other items. (Photographs, 1970s—LA/TW)

Cooling ground pork (for making sausages) at Miller Colony, Montana.
(Photograph, 1970s—LA/TW)

TOP: Boys taking sausages to smokehouse. (Photograph, 1970s—LA/TW)
BOTTOM: Goose butchering day at Old Rockport Colony, Alberta.
(Photograph, 1965—CLA)

Hutterites donating blood at the Red Cross Blood Drive in Lethbridge, Alberta.
(Photographs, 1970—CLA)

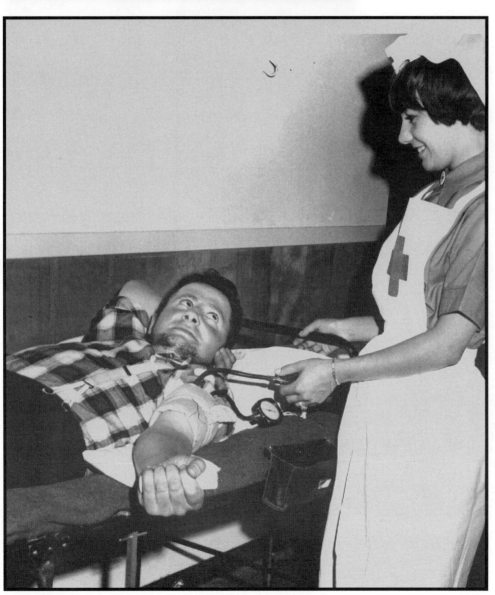

TOP: A fleet of Hutterites' trucks, a common parking lot scene in Lethbridge, Alberta.
(Photograph, 1997—SH)

Hutterite men visiting and exchanging news in Lethbridge, Alberta. In this Canadian city, Thursdays have been dubbed "Black Thursdays," because this is when the largest number of Hutterites come to the city for doctor appointments, business, or to shop.
(Photograph, 1973—CLA)

Student exchange program. Toronto students visiting Rockport Colony in southern Aberta.
(Photograph, 1978—CLA)

Lehrerleit elder. (Photograph— MHLA)

Lehrerleit people walking home after church service. (Photograph, 1994—SH)

TOP: Rearview mirror attached to the side of a unit-house at Rose Valley Colony, Saskatchewan, for extra view. Because the houses are very long, this helps mothers and babysitters keep an eye on small children. It is also a good way to keep an eye on the road and any activities at the shops and garages at the far end of the yard. (Photograph, 1996—SH)

BOTTOM: Modern community kitchen and church at Rose Valley Colony, Saskatchewan. Note the rotating clothesline and the laundry wagon—a standard feature of every family unit. (Photograph, 1996—SH)

Sermons and Songs

Worship services and devotional singing are considered crucial for the spiritual well-being of individuals and the Hutterite community as a whole. Seven days a week, people attend a forty-five to sixty-minute service at either 5:30 p.m. or 6:00 p.m., just before supper, and an hour-and-a-half service on Sunday mornings. The evening services are called *Gebet* (Prayer) and the Sunday morning services are called *Lehr* (Teaching or Sermon). During busy seeding and harvesting seasons, evening worship services are sometimes skipped, but even when they aren't, those who attend are mostly women, who aren't involved with the fieldwork.

When I was about eight, one of my brothers and I were chosen to be the *riefer* (callers) after the second (apprentice) preacher was elected. (All colonies elect an apprentice preacher shortly after a colony branches out.) Because we lived next door to the apprentice preachers's unit, he chose us. As soon as the preacher stepped from his unit and walked up the boardwalks to the church house, we would dash to all the unit-houses, open each door, and shout *"Zum Gebet!"* calling people to church. No bells are rung. Hutterites oppose this practice because they don't want to associate their church with churches "out in the world." For the same reason, no instrumental music is used in church. These kinds of rituals are not considered necessary for worship. At the evening service the preacher is the first to enter the church, and if necessary, he turns on the light. Everyone follows, finding his or her respective seat. Each person sits according to age. At Sunday morning Lehr, Lehrerleit preachers are last to enter the church. For this service, ordained ministers wear a special preacher's coat, a black frock reaching almost to the knees.

Until about the 1980s, the one-room schoolhouse was used as the church. There were no adornment on the walls. At the end of a school day, the blackboards had to be wiped spotless and any student's art hanging on the walls had to be removed. Children sat up front at the school desks. Everyone else sat in the pews, men to the left, women to the right. The schoolteacher's desk was used as the pulpit. The council brethren sat up front, to the right of the preachers, facing everyone. Today, however, the church is usually attached to the communal kitchen, and a soundproof wall between the church and dining hall separates the two. Some churches have a microphone hanging from the ceiling, and via underground wire, the service can be sent to the units of individuals suffering from chronic illnesses or to older people not able to attend. The walls are still bare, and people sit in the same arrangement as always. No boys need dash from house to house, though. The unit-houses are built differently today. In the old style houses, a family lived either in a front or back unit. (Today a family unit extends across the entire width of the long-house, and has both a front and back entrance, giving every family visibility.) In some colonies, rearview mirrors are attached to the sides of the houses so people can have a clear view from one end of the yard to the other. As soon as the preacher steps out the door, everybody sees him. For people not watching and for those on the opposite side of the communal dining hall, a buzzer goes off inside every unit. But even if those cues were not given, people wishing to attend church know the preacher leaves his house at exactly the same time every day. Hutterites are very punctual. For the day to run smoothly, dinner, church, and other daily activities are ordered by the clock.

As soon as everyone is seated, the preacher begins the singing. If both preachers are present, the one standing by leads the singing (the preachers take turns delivering the service). There is a great difference between most Hutterite congregational singing and their singing outside the church. In church, the singing is very formal. The preacher reads one line of the hymn in a singsong, almost chant-like fashion, then the congregation repeats it in unison. Robert Friedmann, a well-known historian, wrote that the women sing in "overloud and rather pressed, shrill voices." He also wrote that he regretted having to say that the singing "does not sound too lovely." A teacher who teaches English school at a colony near Swift Current wasn't so apologetic. "The church singing is very unpleasant," he said. "There is such a big difference in the way people sing in church and outside. The girls have the most pretty voices, and they harmonize

Country music time. (Photograph, 1990s—SH)

beautifully." I was told that this high shrill singing is no longer practiced among most of the Schmiedeleit colonies.

Hutterites do sing a lot, and many are fine singers. Before baptism, a young adult may learn a whole assortment of English hymns and secular songs, and even possess a small musical instrument such as a guitar or harmonica. In recent years, electronic keyboards with all the fancy bells and whistles have become quite popular. Before I left the colony, I owned a guitar, two harmonicas, and a mouth harp. One time one of my older brothers even bought an accordion. My mother wasn't pleased and begged him

continuously to take it back, and he finally did. The harmonica and acoustic guitar are much quieter; unlike the loud accordion, the sound doesn't as easily penetrate the walls of family units. Musical instruments have never been officially allowed in any colony, but today small instruments do not present any great amount of stress or concern. Unless there is a preacher or other stricter elder around, young people play them quite openly inside the home.

It seems as though the first tune played by every Hutterite boy who picks up a guitar plays is "I Walk the Line," "Okie from Muskogee," or any such country classic. And it is uncanny how every

Hutterite's guitar playing from South Dakota to northern Alberta sounds exactly the same. It's as if the "boom chuck, boom chuck" strumming style and the folksy, country twang in their voices was in their genes. The same is true for the girls. With only slight exaggeration, if you've heard one Hutterite sing, you've heard them all.

As for church singing, while it doesn't give me goosebumps as some congregational singing does, I wouldn't say it is "unpleasant." Today, more than anything, I find it interesting. It brings back a flood of bittersweet memories. Hutterite congregational singing is not about singing "nicely." It is about devotion and spiritual expression. This type of congregational singing is actually a very old tradition. Robert Friedmann wrote that it likely originated in the 16th century when many Hutterites were in prison because of their religious beliefs and could not communicate except by singing "overloud." Apparently, there was a certain satisfaction—even pride—that the "world" couldn't really stop those testimonies even in jail! In Peter Riedemann's *Confession of Faith* of 1540, he wrote that all singing "is to be done attentively in the fear of God as inspired by the Spirit of Christ. Where this is not the case, and one sings only for carnal joy, for sweet sounds or for some such reasons, one misuses them [the songs], changing them into what is carnal and worldly, and sings not songs of the spirit, but of the letter." The Hutterites believe that their way of singing in church is a correct interpretation of Riedemann's instructions.

After a couple gets married, the colony provides numerous books such as *Die Geshichtbücher* (chronicles) and *Liederbücher* (songbooks). Among the songbooks they can choose from is *Die Lieder der Hutterischen Brüder* (The Songs of the Hutterian Brethren). This book contains only hymns written by Hutterite forebears. Another one, *Lutherisches Gesangbuch* (Lutheran Songbook), contains 730 German Protestant hymns, written in prose style. The book is indexed alphabetically by melody, subject, and scripture reference, and includes a small selection of prayers. Other songbooks include *Das*

Gesang Büchlein (a collection of hymns used in Church, Sunday school, and in the homes), *Morgen Lieder* (Morning Songs), *Abend Lieder* (Evening Songs), *Begräbnis Lieder* (Funeral Songs), and *Mein Erstes Liederbuch* (My First Songbook).

And there are more. One book, a Mennonite *Gesangbuch,* contains mainly songs for recreational singing. Many young people also have a thick volume containing several hundred popular English hymns, folksongs, gospel songs, and old country and western tunes. Hutterites do not read music, and all their hymnals contain only the texts. All the tunes have been passed on orally from the 16th, 17th, 18th, and 19th centuries. Sources for traditional tunes (songs in German) include court songs, Meistersinger songs, Gregorian chants, and Lutheran chorales. Others include Reformed and free church hymns, secular folk songs, sacred folk songs, American gospel hymns, and, on the extremely secular end, popular country and western songs. Because of the oral tradition, the tunes vary from printed sources as well as from colony to colony. In church, people sing only in

Lehrerleit boys enjoying some music. (Photograph—SH)

unison and with extreme slowness, whereas in the home their singing is more relaxed in tempo and attitude.

Today, many young people own portable tape or CD players and are quick to learn soft songs by the Rankin Family, Ricky Scaggs, and other country music or pop stars. Some even hang large posters of their favorite singer on their

Young Schmiedeleit women at Forest River Colony, North Dakota, singing at school Christmas program. (Photograph, 1978—TW)

bedroom wall. When I was in my teens, people rarely listened to anything but country music, but I began tuning to rock and roll stations on my transistor radio and soon was attempting to sing songs by Bob Seger, Gerry Rafferty—even the BeeGees. However, this kind of secular singing was not and never has been sanctioned by the elders. For the most part, it is done in private or at a social gathering for young people.

So, on the one hand there is the traditional Hutterite church music—the classical stuff if you will—and the *other* music, bordering more and more on the secular, where "singing nicely" is important. While Peter Riedemann's instruction on singing is still held up as true doctrine, those singing English hymns, gospel songs, and secular songs, hardly consider it, if at all. Most young people don't even know about Peter Riedemann's instruction. In any case, I don't think people singing in church are keen on purposely singing loud. By now it is a cultural characteristic, and the

songs, expressed without musical accompaniment, lend themselves to this kind of church singing.

After the singing, the preacher rises from his chair and opens the service, which begins with the same words every time: "Der Frieden des Hernn, die liebe Gottes, und die Gemeinshaft Seines Heiligen Geistes, sei mit uns alle in diese gegenwärtige Abend (Morgen) Stunde." ["May the Peace of the Lord, the Love of God, and the Community of His Holy Spirit be with us all in this Evening (Morning) Hour."] After a short memorized opening, he opens his black handwritten and hand-bound sermon book and reads the sermon. The Hutterite sermons, all of which are in High German, are read in a monotonous tone, a bit like a litany. These sermons follow a seasonal pattern, some leading up to major Holidays such as Easter, Christmas, and Pentecost. Each of the Christian holidays that Hutterites celebrate has one or more complimentary sermons from which the preacher can choose. There are about 350 different sermons in use among the Hutterites. Most of these sermons were written by Hutterite forebears in the 16th and 17th centuries. Each preacher has 150 to 200 sermons in his collection.

Traditionally, a preacher painstakingly hand-copied all the sermons he used. He may also have given someone close to him, who had exceptionally good handwriting, the honor of copying sermons for him. In the 1970s, my father, not a preacher, wrote many sermons for the apprentice preacher mentioned earlier. The colony's bookbinder then bound the sermons and delivered them to the preacher. This tradition of hand-copying sermons and other writings goes as far back as 1585 or further, culminating in the work of the Ehrenpreis period when the Ehrenpreis team, around 1650, produced the bulk of the material. Through the process of hand-copying the material, the writer becomes intimately familiar with the literature. Today, however, pressed for time, most preachers use the photocopier for this job.

Most preachers don't improvise on the sermon much, if at all, but they may—especially those with good oral skills—stop now and then to address the congregation and interject something, perhaps putting the sermon into the context of contemporary life. At least one minister, Jacob Kleinsasser, a former *vorsteher* (bishop) of the Schmiedeleit, laid aside traditions and wrote a few of his own sermons a few years ago and improvised a lot while preaching. While this seemed acceptable in some Schmiedeleit communities, the Lehrerleit and Dariusleit were hardly impressed, and were even alarmed. They fear that writing new sermons—even rewriting old ones—is tampering with the doctrine upon which the Hutterite faith is founded upon. To be fair to Kleinsasser, he did write two introductions to sermons for events that didn't yet have fitting introductions assigned to them: *Predigerstimm* (preacher election), and *Danksagung* (Thanksgiving). Also, he has translated a considerable amount of material from German to English.

After the sermon there is a prayer that usually lasts about ten minutes. With everyone kneeling on the floor, the preacher spontaneously prays for the spiritual and material welfare of the community, and sometimes even for individuals. However, no prayer is ever complete without giving thanks for blessings received.

I remember one summer when I was sixteen or seventeen. It didn't rain for a long while and the crops desperately needed moisture. Finally, one day it rained. Everyone was in great spirits. That evening, with the fieldwork and all other work halted because of the rain, practically everybody made it to church—even those who habitually found excuses not to go (by dragging their work out just long enough until everybody was gathered in the church). Every colony has a few lax individuals who can always find menial tasks to do just before church. Anyway, on the day the rain fell, the pews were filled to capacity. When the preacher thanked God for the rain, waves of emotion flooded my soul. I was happy. The skies were suddenly bluer and the air was crisper. I remember going to the communal bake house in the evening, where we (the boys) had a nine-inch color television set hidden in the rafters. Radio (for entertainment) and television are forbidden in Hutterite communities. Although I watched a show with the boys, I felt terribly guilty that evening. When God is very personal in a person's life, one really is compelled to seek to please Him. Although I did not carry it through entirely, this experience made me understand how inner and outer service to God are related. Those people who later in the evening sang songs of devotion from their Liederbücher, so that you could hear their singing fill the cooled air, probably had light hearts when they went to bed.

Following the prayer, the preacher says a few closing words and people file out. The preacher is the last to go out the door.

The daily sermon and prayer (Gebet) is each colony's shorter version of the worship service. At Sunday morning Lehr, the prayer is followed by yet another sermon, which is usually a bit longer than the first one. In addition, at the end of the service, a few more verses are sung, then the preacher dismisses everybody. When there is business to discuss (usually this follows Gebet rather than Lehr), he briefly turns to the council brethren and tells them to remain sitting. If the discussion needs the participation of all the baptized brethren (men only), he will give them notice too, and they remain sitting.

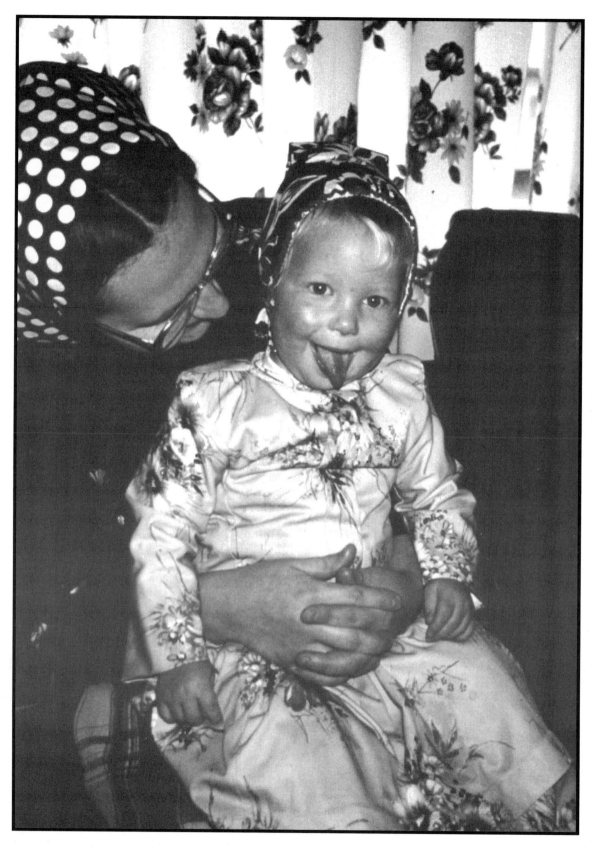

A Lehrerleit mother and daughter. (Photograph, 1980s—LG)

Life Cycles, Traditions, and Stages of Hutterite Life

The cycles of Hutterite life include common events such as birth, baptism, marriage, and death. But there are other events, rites of passages and seasons of life, that overlap the major ones. Life in mainstream North American society is often anything but predictable, but a Hutterite's life, if one stays in the colony, is very likely to follow a set pattern because the community eschews social change and people don't follow careers outside the agrarian community. "It's like a chain," a Hutterite minister said of religious traditions. "As long as you have the links together, it's still a chain. But once you start breaking the links, it's no longer a chain."

Age and life cycles are used to order Hutterite society. Hutterites believe that God established a divine order among people, which requires a hierarchy of relationships. God is lord over the man, the man is overseer of the woman, and the elder is overseer of the young. At the dinner table, in church, and in school, people always sit ranked by age, males on one side of the room, and females on the other. At the end of a church service, people file out in order of birth, the oldest woman following the youngest boy. When I was growing up, age even determined who sat in the middle when we got into a single truck seat. The older person always got the window seat, no questions asked.

Children

The births of children, unless born out of wedlock, are not severely disruptive events in Hutterite society. Neither is death of the elderly, because it is assumed that "the Lord giveth and the Lord taketh away." Birth is expected and experienced regularly among the colony's married people. Today, most Hutterite children are born in hospitals. Women work right up until the baby is born, and then they go on maternity leave for six weeks. During this time the new mothers get special attention; their meals, made specifically for them, are delivered to their homes. After six weeks of total leave they receive another three weeks of semi-leave. During that period they are exempted from all work, but participate in all other communal activities. Always on call when group work is required, there is usually a babysitter (young girl), a retired older woman, or grandmother available to help. Children begin kindergarten at two-and-a-half or three years of age, so from then on, daycare is provided. Women sometimes do leave the children at home alone, but rarely for longer than an hour at a time.

Hutterite children are wanted and loved. Very seldom is there a shortage of siblings, cousins, or other children for an individual to play with. And there are always adults around, including uncles and aunts, to entertain, hug, sweet-talk the child, and bounce on their knee, making the child feel wanted and special. Adults generally do not show their affection to each other in public, but they are not shy in expressing fondness toward children. I have sometimes observed a roomful of adults conversing about serious matters, then do a complete turn when a young child was brought into their midst. Suddenly the child was the center of attention, providing entertainment, however seemingly trivial and silly, for the entire lot. Children are considered blessings and gifts from God. And

TOP: Lehrerleit woman with baby.
(Photograph, 1990s—SH)

BOTTOM: Lehrerleit babies.
(Photograph—LA/TW)

they aren't baptized or dedicated. Hutterites believe that children are safe in Jesus Christ until they reach an age of accountability. It is the responsibility of the parents to love the child but also to discipline appropriately for misbehavior (later this also becomes the German school teacher's responsibility) so that the child might grow up respecting older people and the community. It can be a very disruptive experience for a colony if parents fail to discipline their children, teach them the values of the community, and show them how to respect their teachers and elders.

As mentioned earlier, at two-and-a-half or three years of age, children enter kindergarten. This, and regular German and English schools until age fifteen or sixteen (ages vary) constitute the formal schooling most Hutterites receive. But seldom does education end there. Being proficient farmers and sharp businesspeople, members often go to trade seminars and take courses in animal husbandry, welding, electrical work, electronics, or any other required training for the respective occupation in the community. That aside, reaching fifteen years of age (fourteen in Lehrerleit colonies) is an important rite of passage because it is the beginning of adulthood. While full adulthood status is only achieved with marriage or baptism, to a degree, around fifteen years of age a person begins adult life. Now, counted as a member of the colony's labor force, the young adult no longer eats with the children but with the adults.

(Photograph—LA/TW)

49

TOP: Lehrerleit children playing with battery operated toy. (Photograph, 1990s—SH)

BOTTOM: School children at Rose Valley Colony, Saskatchewan. (Photograph, 1990s—SH)

The Young Adult Years

During the young adult years (between the end of schooling and baptism), it is common for people to leave the community and work outside the colony for awhile or hang a bit loose, possessing a radio or musical instrument, playing sports, earning private money by working outside the colony for a neighbor, or trapping, etc. Unless these activities become disruptive to the community, they are somewhat overlooked. There are consequences for such transgressions. The usual punishment for young people is standing up in church and being reprimanded by the preacher.

In my teens, I trapped foxes and coyotes, as did some of the other young adults in our community. In the late 1970s and early 1980s, fur prices were very high, so some of us had more pocket money than usual. However, with money came other things the elders did not approve of. We had many of the latest country and western and pop music tapes, which we listened to on portable stereo systems. As I mentioned earlier, the boys even had a top-quality Toshiba color television that we bought by pooling our money, communal style. Anybody who had not contributed financially had no say over what we watched, because we always decided what to watch by voting. It was like buying shares. A few months after we had purchased the television set, one of my cousins, upon returning to the colony after being away for two years, wanted in, so he paid $45, which was disbursed to all the original shareholders. After that, he too had voting privileges. We secretly watched shows such as *Three's Company*, *Charlie's Angels*, *Dallas*, and *Hockey Night in Canada*.

At age fourteen or fifteen, young people usually start coming together in "the crowd," which is a term used for a gathering of youth for the purpose of social interaction, whether with people from their own colony or with youth from other colonies.

About that time most young adults start dating, which is not dating in the typical sense of going out to supper or to enjoy some entertainment. The community would not allow

it? Where would they go, and how would they get there? The Hutterite terms for dating—which to an extent includes the early stages of courting (going steady)—are *diene youg'n* (chasing girls) and *ummrlauf'n* (running around). The latter term also includes girls. These words, in their English translated contexts, don't aptly describe dating, because a date could be as simple as going for a walk or sitting in a dark corner holding hands, talking, and kissing. On a typical date however, a couple meets in a private room, preferably with a cot or bed on which to sit or lie on (most Hutterites don't have sofas in their homes). Sometimes several dating couples will use the room simultaneously, each minding their own business, on separate cots. And so, usually with the lights off, the couple "dates," often in horizontal position. I was told that this is not universally practiced among the Schmiedeleit, but I do know it is among the Lehrerleit. I suspect that most young people of all three leit date that way. The Amish, who apparently date in similar fashion, have a more fitting term: Bundling. Bundling is a courtship practice carried over from colonial American times when houses were cold and a young man would visit a woman in bed, fully clad. As you might expect, Hutterite elders are not exactly at ease with this practice and often admonish the youth to be careful. People will seldom talk about this courting practice to an outsider—I think out of embarrassment or fear that it might be misconstrued as being promiscuous. No doubt, this practice can be sexually tempting and even lead to promiscuity. Twenty or thirty years ago, pregnancies among young people were rare. However, the higher rate of pre-marital pregnancies occurring in Hutterite communities today suggests a sexual liberation has taken place. Yet I do not think bundling can be blamed. Pre-marital pregnancies among Hutterites are a sign of the times and where Hutterites find themselves today in relation to the outside world. Hutterite youth have access to magazines, movies, and music videos. The sexual images portrayed through these mediums are very powerful. Whatever the reality may be in actual practice, however, all Hutterites still hold that sexual relations should occur only within marriage.

A Lehrerleit couple. (Photograph, early 1980s—SH)

The author, Samuel Hofer, while still living in the colony, proudly displaying his furs.
(Photograph, 1981—SH)

The author, while still living in the colony, drawing cartoons. (Photograph, 1981—SH)

TOP: A young Lehrerleit woman showing her personal belongings inside *shronk* (chest of drawers). At age fourteen or fifteen, young people in the colony receive either a chest of drawers or a hope chest. This coincides with the beginning of adulthood. (Photograph, 1980s— SH)

BOTTOM: A young man's basement bedroom. (Photograph, 1994—SH)

A Schmiedeleit couple. (Photograph, 1970s—LA/TW)

Baptism

Hutterites become full members of their church community upon getting baptized, usually in their twenties. There is no formal rule for the exact age a person asks for baptism, other than that one must be at least nineteen years of age. When a candidate accepts baptism, he or she is believed to have received the supernatural gift of the Holy Spirit through obedience and submission and thereafter has more power and responsibility over those who have not yet taken these vows. Baptism is one of the most important events in a Hutterite's life and marks a relinquishing of old ways upon full confession of faith. While it does signify a rebirth in Jesus Christ, equal emphasis is given to becoming a member, synonymous with believer, in the Communal Church. One's faith in Jesus Christ, as the Hutterite Catechism states, must be expressed through the love and service of the community. Before baptism is granted, individuals' behavior is monitored for a full year to ascertain that the candidates are serious with this spiritual undertaking. Before baptism, which always occurs just before Easter, the *onholtr* or *täuflinge* (baptismal candidates) are required to spend six Sunday afternoons with the elders (men only), who indoctrinate and admonish them in the tenets of the Hutterite faith. The day before the baptism a special service takes place during which the candidates and the whole community are once more admonished regarding the significance of Christian baptism. In fact, a series of special sermons are preached in the days leading up to the event. Following the service, the candidates recite numerous scriptural verses, which include the Hutterite Catechism and the *taufshpruch* (baptismal-poem), a 161-line confession of faith. This is an intensely serious yet joyous occasion, for now a person takes his or her place as a member of the church. Furthermore, after the confession of all sins to the head preacher, followed by baptism, a person starts life anew, having been reborn in Christ. The slate is wiped clean, and all previous sins, however severe, are considered forgiven. Now however, as a "brother" or "sister" of the community, the members take on new responsibilities, which include admonishing others when necessary, and being a witness to their faith.

After baptism, it is also necessary for the members to partake in *Abendmahl Lehr* (the Eucharist) at Easter time.

For full members of the church, transgressions such as earning private money, getting inebriated, hitting or verbally abusing another member, and so on, warrant harsher punishments than those given to people not yet baptized. A person is put on probation called *unfrieden* (without peace). During this time, the member does not attend church nor eat with the rest of the people. This type of church discipline usually last about two weeks. For extreme transgressions such as adultry and misappropriating community funds, a member gets shunned (excommunicated temporarily). The individual doesn't actually leave the colony. However, no member of the church can refer to the shunned individual as a church member. He or she is not considered to be under the covenant of the church. This type of discipline—"silent treatment"—typically lasts about two weeks also.

Marriage

Once baptized, a person can ask for marriage, but only with another church member in good standing. As far as I know, no interfaith marriage has ever occurred within the Hutterite church. In fact, the mere idea might present an oxymoron. The saying "You're either in the ark, or you're not" can aptly be applied here. Being in the ark means being in the colony spiritually. If a person left the colony, got married outside then wished to return to the colony with his or her spouse, the marriage would not be recognized unless both became members of the church. I do not know of any such marriage, because it is rare for people to join the Hutterite community. Many people are attracted to this way of life, but few can make the necessary sacrifices. Submissiveness to the will of the community and the church, the dissolution of all individual material wealth, and adopting the traditional lifestyle are usually too difficult. Except for the Society of Brothers in the Eastern United States, which I'll deal with later in a chapter called "When East Met West," only a few individuals or families have joined Hutterite colonies since they

Cedar and redwood heart chests, made by a young Hutterite man to give to his sweetheart. (Photograph, 1997—SH)

settled in North America. While the exact numbers were not available to me, I did conclude, from my research and conversations with people, that no more than twenty individuals or families from mainstream society have joined Hutterites communities in the last one hundred years. Some of these have resulted in unhappy situations, primarily because converts, who apparently didn't completely conform to the Hutterite way, eventually influenced other members in such a way that they ended up leaving the colony together.

Marriage usually takes place soon after baptism and is an informal requirement for full participation in the community. Most Hutterites expect to get married and have a family. I think that very few people would actually choose not to get married.

Wedding traditions vary slightly among the three Leit, so I will give only the basic traditions here. Traditionally, the woman moves to the man's community. The reason for that, since theirs is a patriarchal (sociologists use the word "patrilocal") society, is that men typically occupy positions of authority, while most women do not. This helps, although not entirely, to establish congruent patterns of management within a community and ensures that jobs pertaining to the operations of the colony are somewhat elected according to age. Women—this is not to say that I think it is fair—can adapt more readily to the "management and positions politics" of another colony, primarily because they are not directly involved.

A couple asking to get married usually becomes engaged one or two weeks before the wedding. On a weekday (Sunday among the Schmiedeleit), the prospective bride groom, accompanied by his father and one or more close relatives, travel to the woman's colony and deliver a letter from their preacher to the preacher at the prospective bride's colony, formally requesting that consent for the marriage be given. (If the woman is from the same colony some of these steps may not be necessary.) If the preacher, the young woman's parents, and she assent, an engagement service is held in the church that same day, witnessed by the entire community. The prospective bride wears a blue brocade wedding dress, featuring a carnation or other similar flower design. There is no veil as in the typical North American style, and the bride wears her head covering (kerchief) as usual. The bridegroom wears a black Sunday suit (which his fiancée has made for him) with a white shirt and black tie. The engagement vows are similar to traditional wedding vows of most Christian churches in mainstream North America: affirmations that they will accept their marital obligations in health and in sickness, happiness and in sorrow, and so forth.

After the engagement ceremony and a short supper, the couple retires to the home of the bride's parents where, starting with parents and kin, they serve a liqueur-type mixed drink or a small glass of wine. The sitting room has been lined with chairs and benches for visitors to sit on. Ever practical, cardboard has been placed on the floors so that the frequent traffic from visitors will not mar the floor finish. As friends, kin, and colony members take their drink, they make a toast and offer their wishes and advice. I remember how at a cousin's wedding I tried hard to come up with something to say. Most people allowed a simple "Good Luck" or "The Best of Health to You" to suffice. I wanted to say something profound, something the couple would not easily forget or hadn't heard before. But what was I to say? I was only eighteen. What possible advice could I give them about marriage? I knew nothing about it. I remember saying something about God being full of Grace and that I hoped they would always live in His Peace. Well, it was original!

After the toasting, at about 7:30 in the evening, the bell at the community hall rings and an *aufreden hulba* (engagement ceremony) gets underway in the community dining hall. The Lehreleit call this a *stübela* or shivaree. The sitting arrangements vary among the Leit, but generally, the couple take their place, sitting perpendicular to the rest of the tables or benches, facing the entrance. A little clearing in front of the couple provides a space for those wishing to take the floor to sing a solo or to tell a joke or two. For about two hours, the community engages in singing *huchzeit lieder* (festive hymns or songs) in German and English, which people read from

hand-copied homemade books. One of the many different compilations of Hutterite songs include one volume called *Hochzeit Lieder*. People wanting to have a turn singing a solo, reciting humorous verses or songs such as "*Ich Bin Der Doktor Eisnbort*" ("I am Doctor Ironbeard") or a funny "Dear John" letter, telling jokes or performing a short skit, must first report to the chairman who organizes the entertainment.

Around 9:30 p.m. the couple takes a break and returns to the home of the bride's parents. A few minutes later the bell rings again and everyone returns to the dining hall where lunch is served. (In Hutterite terms, lunch refers to all coffee breaks and snack breaks.) Lehrerleit usually serve potato chips, ice cream, ham and cheese sandwiches, a banana, and coffee. After lunch, the couple retires to the apartment once more. Most of the older people go home after the lunch, but the younger people continue the party in an unused unit or in the schoolroom and continue to sing and socialize into the wee hours. Usually, the engaged couple joins them. After the elders have gone home, people who are able to play a musical instrument will bring it out and play a few songs.

A day or two before the wedding, the groom with a brother or friend will drive to the bride's colony once more, to pick up the bride and (always on a Saturday) make the trip to the groom's colony. Of course, if the couple is from the same colony, this trip isn't necessary. Usually, the bride's siblings and parents return with them. The couple and a sister or brother drive ahead, in the truck hauling the young woman's belongings. Among these belongings are wedding gifts and a dowry from her natal colony, which includes her clothes and fabrics, sewing machine, bedding and bedroom furniture. She may also have other furniture, such as upholstered benches, tables, and chairs that she finished in anticipation of her marriage. The groom's colony has prepared for their arrival. The couple are expected to arrive before 5:00 p.m., in time to have some refreshments, then attend the evening church service, which also pertains to this occasion. Arriving about this time are also other invited guests, including the bride's sister and brother-in-laws and their children. Traditions vary between colonies concerning who is automatically invited

TOP: Hutterite
engagement, a
communal affair.
(Photograph,
1980—HM)

BOTTOM:
**Engaged Lehrerleit
couples at shivaree
(engagement
party).** (Photograph,
1990—SH)

Lehrerleit girls at engagement party, deciding which hymn to sing next. (Photograph, 1989—SH)

and who is not. Often this depends on the particular colony's preacher. After supper, the couple serves a liqueur-type mixed drink or a small glass of wine, this time to the members of the groom's community. Following that, another hulba or stübela takes place, which is virtually the same as the one held a few days earlier in the bride's home colony.

On Sunday morning, the church service begins at 9:30 a.m.—even earlier in some colonies. The bride and groom sit near each other on an aisle seat on their respective side. She wears a blue dress, much like the one she wore at the engagement ceremony, and he wears a black Sunday suit and white shirt with a black tie. The service is much like any other Sunday Lehr, including the prayer, and is about the same length: one-and-a-half hours. It is selected from traditional Hutterite text and Bible citations, and it centers on the responsibilities of marriage and spiritual life. The theme focuses on submissiveness of the wife to the husband and the submissiveness of the husband to the church and Christ, admonishing both to lead each other to a life in God. At the end of the service, after a few introductory words

about the couple and their union, the two are called to stand together in front of the preacher.

One vow is unique to the Hutterite faith. With both their right hands clasped together, the groom is asked to affirm that should he "suffer shipwreck of his faith," he not ask his wife and children to follow him in his wrong ways, and that "on behalf of his woman, he not cause the community any trouble with the authorities," if he should desire to leave the colony. The bride is asked if she, having heard her betrothed's good intentions, "desires to accept him in good will without complaint."

With their wedding vows said, the couple returns to their seats. No kiss is exchanged in church, no veil is removed, and no ring is given. All these, according to Hutterite faith, belong to the ways of the "world." However, aside from the church ceremony, the couple is permitted to kiss anytime they choose to do so throughout the entire remaining wedding ceremonies, including the shivarees. Following additional scriptures, the prayer, a blessing, and singing, the service is finished. Outside, the now married couple rejoins, and with friends and well-wishers congratulating

Hutterite wedding photograph. (Photograph, 1980s—SH)

them, they return to the home of the groom's family unit to wait for the dining hall bell, calling everyone to the wedding meal.

Typically, Hutterites eat fast, as if there was no time to lose. The wedding meal, however, is a leisurely and drawn-out affair. The long varnished tables are covered with a white tablecloth, and special plates and bowls are used. As with all meals, each person folds his or her hands, and one of the elders recites a short prayer (blessing), then the meal begins. The meal is the same as on any other Sunday: traditional egg noodles, stewed broiler chickens or stewed duck, gooseberry pudding, and other items. At this meal, adults are served two or three rounds of beer, which the *shencker* (servers) distribute to the tables. The children are served soft drinks. The older children, those nearing Leit age (fourteen or fifteen), may be served one small glass of beer as

well. At this meal and celebrations following in the afternoon, men serve the food and drink. While the regular cooks (whose week the wedding happens to fall on) are not relieved of their cooking duties, a crew of men is assigned to help them. People, like they always do, sit in groups of four at the long tables, and the food is distributed accordingly. Except for the newlyweds' and their families' headtables, which are situated at the far end of the hall, perpendicular to all the rest, the women sit on one side and the men on the other. Because there are so many guests, the rule of seating according to age is waived somewhat. This meal is the first and last time the couple will officially sit together as man and wife at a communal meal in the dining hall.

After the wedding meal, the elder recites a verse of thanks and the people file out. The newlyweds return to the home of the groom's parents. Guests drop by to visit and look at the wedding cakes and wedding gifts. This is also the time when the young people (at least in Lehrerleit colonies) come forth with their cameras for a photo session. The layered wedding cakes, which appear to be getting fancier and have increasingly more layers every few years, are placed on a table. Beside the cakes are all the wedding cards the couple have received. While wedding photos were rare thirty years ago, today most Hutterites take many pictures. As far as I know, no professional photographers are hired. Not yet.

At 1:30 p.m. the *huchzeit* (wedding celebration) resumes once more in the dining hall. The preacher begins the celebrations with the refrain: *"Am Dritten Tag Ein Hochzeit War."* ("On the Third Day Was a Wedding.") The song is about the wedding Jesus attended with his disciples and his mother, during which he turned water into wine. All afternoon, with an intermission about halfway through, people sing hymns while drinking and snacking leisurely. Lehrerleit and Dariusleit sing only German songs at this event. Schmiedeleit sing in both German and English. Usually served are beer or wine, soft drinks, peanuts, potato chips, fruit, cake and ice cream, and other snacks. Except during prayers and songs lead by the minister, people go from table to table to have a drink (toast) with friends and relatives and, of course, the bride and groom. Towards the end of the afternoon, around 5:00 p.m., the huchzeit ends with the preacher leading one last song. The business manager's wife has prepared treat packets, and everyone gets one to take home.

There is more visiting in the evening after supper. In the summer, colony members and guests (usually the younger folk) may also pile into passenger vans and go off for an evening of "looking at the crops" in the country around the colony. While most colonies loosely practice this outing tradition, some have it during the week, before the wedding, instead of after.

Later in the evening, guests, family, and friends join the newlyweds one more time to eat the wedding cake in the home of the groom's parents. After that, the couple retires to their own unit, which in the weeks leading up to this has been transformed into a fully functional living space, to the same standards and modernity as all other identical family units in the community.

The following morning, the couple attends breakfast in the dining hall, but now the husband returns to his respective seat at the long table, and the wife takes hers among the women, sitting according to her age. They are exempted from any work on that day. Later in the day, the guests from other colonies pack up and head home.

The Hutterite woman "marrying away" to a new colony gains a husband, which is very important, but she loses the comfort, security, and emotional stability of her previous life and relationships. In addition, she has to adjust to a new geographical environment, new relatives and colony members, and very often different "ways of doing things." There is also a shift in how she is perceived. Whereas before marriage she was still more or less considered one of the *diene* (girls), now she is one of the *weiber* (women). When Hutterites refer to the women, they usually mean those women already married. The same applies to the men, but not as extensively. The younger boys are referred to as the *buebm* (boys); sometimes even the baptized and as yet unmarried men are called *buebm*. More often than not, however, a baptized man is referred to as one of the *monsleit* (men folk). When referring to all the men together, including those over fifteen right up to those around sixty, they are designated as the men folk. As for "elders," this word translates to *de olten* (the old ones). The older women, or those of grandmother age, are called the *ankele*, which in Hutterish language literally means "grandmothers." I give these details to show that people are ranked or categorized not only according to age, but also by their baptismal and marital status. Interestingly, a bachelor is often called an *olter bua* (old boy), and an unmarried older woman is referred to as an *olta dien* (old girl).

The newly married young woman in a Hutterite community is often in a vulnerable position at first, because Hutterite marriage also serves to help the man maintain his dominant position and emphasize the dependency of his new wife. Relatives, including her husband, however work hard to make her part of their family, and in time she adjusts to her new community. She will visit her family "back home," sometimes for weeks at a time, but unless a sister also marries someone from her new colony, she will never again live in the same colony as her parents and other biological family members.

Marriage—for the man at least—serves to help him acquire or maintain a prominent position in the community. Through marriage, he obtains a new status and role, giving him an informal eligibility for work assignments requiring more responsibility than positions allotted to single men. Just as importantly, he gains his own home and a loyal partner who will support him both spiritually and physically, and likely bear him a family. The woman also gains. Aside from the obvious benefits of having her own home and possibly a family, she gains, through her husband, a better means of having her input in the colony's affairs brought to the meetings and voting circles, albeit indirectly. Her husband is likely to also take her needs into consideration when voting on any issue.

Dariusleit women at Espanola Colony, near Spokane, Washington. (Photograph, 1980s—BM)

Lehrerleit women and children. (Photograph, 1990s—SH)

"Don't shoot! It's a sin!" A Lehrerleit woman warns a researcher (around 1950) that according to one of the Ten Commandments, taking pictures was forbidden: "Thou shall not make a graven image." Although having a picture taken was taboo, possessing a photograph once it was taken (by an outsider) carried little negative sanction. Today, although picture-taking is still considered a sin by some older Hutterites, many young people in the colony own their own cameras and take photographs regularly. (Photograph—JE/TW)

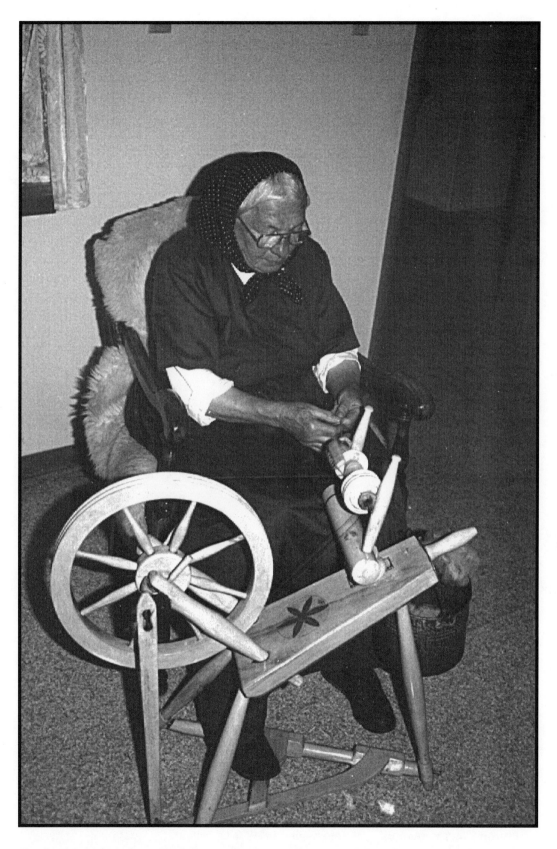

Dariusleit ankela (grandmother) spinning, at Surprise Creek Colony, near Stanford, Montana. (Photograph, 1983—BM)

Paul Knels (1904-1978) was the last of the Knels among the Hutterites, and the name is now extinct in the colonies. It can be traced to 1783, when a widow named Lisel Knels and her two sons (from the Low German Menonites in Prussia) joined the Hutterites at Vishenka, in the Ukraine. Mr. Knels lived at Huron Colony, Manitoba. (Photograph—LA/TW)

Middle and Old Age

As I mentioned earlier, the work, social, and familial patterns in Hutterite community life serve to provide opportunities for all members to grow into or out of respective roles. During their childbearing years, women continue with "women's work," which includes baking, cooking, canning, and so on. Except for six to nine weeks of maternity leave after bearing a child, women aren't exempted from any work duties relegated to their age group.

Around forty-five years of age, women can retire from cooking, baking, and garden work, but unless a woman has health problems, she continues doing some work in these areas. All women, which includes senior women to a degree, are still required to perform some duties, such as dish washing, cleaning, pea shelling, making noodles, preparing food for preserving, and butchering. Usually when women retire from cooking, they become kindergarten teachers. A typical colony usually has two or three women of that age to take turns running the kindergarten.

The head cook doesn't necessarily retire at the regular retirement age. She may go on serving in this position for several years after. This position requires considerable management skill and the ability to get along with people. The head cook, as with all positions, is elected by the (male) council, but with much influence from the women. She is required to work efficiently with male leadership. Aside from supervising kitchen duties, she also oversees some of the women's work. Another position held by a woman is the *schneider* or head seamstress, who is responsible for ordering fabrics from wholesalers and allotting each family in the community their share. She is usually the financial manager's wife and is responsible for allotting fruit, candy, snack food, and other items bought by the colony from time to time. She also stocks a supply of basic medicines, such as aspirins, ointments, and first aid supplies.

A woman's power and influence, providing she is in good health, is usually greatest during old age, and depending on her ability and personality, she can continue to influence the women's subculture and thus the life of the colony. Most of this unofficial influence, however, comes through her adult sons living in the same colony. And if she happens to be the mother of the first preacher or the financial manager, her influence may be even greater, because then she is in a better position yet to influence colony decisions. A man, eligible to become the financial manager, may be disregarded for this position by the brethren if his wife is known to lack initiative and leadership skills. This proves that women play a larger role in the colony's affairs than stereotypes suggest.

The men more or less work their way up, increasingly taking on leadership roles with age. Starting in the fields, working as physical laborers or operating tractors and equipment, they get elected (according to age and aptitude) to stock jobs, blacksmith, carpenter, teacher, and so on.

(Photograph, 1970s—LA/TW)

The financial manager is usually an older member, who has gone through various stages of management. There is no set age for when a Hutterite becomes "elderly." A man may give up his leadership position as boss or financial manager, but continue serving on the council, as a trustee. In church, the council brethren sit to the right of the preachers, facing the congregation. As long as a brother is mentally and physically able, he continues to serve in that position, and his input is according to his ability. A preacher holds his position for life and continues preaching as long as

69

he feels he can, often into old age. As long as his voice and eyesight for reading the sermons are good, he will go on preaching. However, if he begins slipping up when reciting the long prayer, or if he forgets part of it, it is a sign that he should stop preaching, and the colony may request another preacher.

The Final Rite

From the cradle to the grave, a Hutterite's life has its varied and timely rhythms within the integrated community. While the very old have limited influence in colony economics or management, they maintain a certain importance as teachers and as bearers of traditions. Young people are taught that it is their duty to respect the elderly and what they stand for. In Hutterite society, the elderly are well taken care of and continue to live surrounded by their families and friends whom they have known all their lives, and are able to experience their declining years as "golden years," free from financial and social worries. When the burden of taking care of someone becomes too much, relatives (always women) from other colonies will arrive to help, taking turns as caregivers. When I was in my teens, my mother's aunt had a stroke and most of her body was paralyzed. She lived for five years after the stroke and even improved slightly at one point, but she remained in bed and under constant care. She had no children of her own. However, she had many relatives in several colonies, who took turns caring for her.

With the certainty of salvation, if a person has remained true to the faith and lived communally, death is not something feared. Hutterites consider death a natural transition from one life (corporal and temporary) to another (heavenly and eternal). On earth, people are merely pilgrims, and all of life is a preparation for death. It is always sad when a person dies as a child or before reaching old age—and even more so if a person dies suddenly. But there is also a certain relaxed attitude about it. "He (or she) is so lucky" is often the comment. "He has it so good now." Sometimes there is even envy. I remember on more than one occasion, at the death of a child

somewhere, individuals even remarked that they wished that they too had died as a child, because then they would have been spared the many temptations of sin and the tribulations of life, and thus be assured eternal paradise, even though this life would have been shortened.

The dying person is supported by praying, singing, and conversations with people close to him or her. Hutterites try to avoid hospital deaths, insisting that death belongs to the dying and those who love them, not to the medical establishment. They also dislike death that is postponed or sudden death, which cheats individuals of the opportunity to say farewell to their family and friends and to put their life in order.

Recently I received a telephone call from a man from a Dariusleit colony near Swift Current whom I had met only briefly fifteen years earlier when a few of the young men from our colony rented a car and traveled to several colonies to play hockey. His father was in the hospital because of kidney failure. This man and his sister were taking turns staying near their father, keeping him company as he lay dying. I cannot divulge here what spiritual significance this experience had for me or claim that I might have had some role to fill, but for some reason, the man needed a break from the hospital atmosphere. We met and then, only an hour after we had returned from drinking a beer, he phoned me again, this time to say his father had just passed away. It was a moving experience. But what stuck in my mind most of all was an anecdote he had related to me. Earlier, his sister and he had said some prayers and sung some traditional songs for their father. As they sang, some elderly people in nearby hospital rooms had slowly made their way along the hallway to their door. They had tears in their eyes. Tears of joy. They were Mennonites, and still remembered those old German hymns from their younger days, but no longer sang them today. I can imagine—or maybe I can't—the comfort their father had, hearing those, which he had learned by rote as a child and sung all his life in church and in his home. The hymns that connected him to his faith, his Hutterite life and heritage—his very existence.

At the death of an individual, the colony manager immediately "puts in a call" to a few colonies where the closest relatives live. This

TOP: Pallbearers. (Photograph—TW)
BOTTOM: The Friedhof (cemetery), at Rockport, South Dakota, where
Joseph and Michael Hofer, the last Hutterite Martyrs, are buried.
(Photograph—LA/TW)

activates the phoning tree. Within hours, many colonies are notified. Those people choosing to go to the funeral cease all work and travel to share in the mourning and funeral activities. Unless a person is directly related or needs to go along as driver, usually only baptized people go. However, this is a loosely held rule. It is not always practiced. Within a short time, women and unmarried girls from nearby colonies arrive to help prepare huge quantities of food, and bake traditional sweet *leicht zwieback* (funeral buns). Depending on the status of the deceased, a colony may receive several hundred mourners.

As elsewhere, the deceased is taken to a local undertaker. Then the body is returned to the colony and to the family unit of the deceased, dressed in traditional Hutterite clothing. Friends and relatives take turns sitting with mourning family members. The wake continues for two days and two nights, amid singing, prayers, reflective silence, and conversation. Many of the songs are from the Hutterite hymnal *Begräbnis Lieder* (Burial Songs), including songs such as "O Lord, Blissful Departure" and "Man, Think Daily Upon Your Mortality." On the day of the funeral most work stops and people take the day off. The deceased is placed in a wooden coffin made by the colony carpenter, then taken to the church for the *leicht* (funeral service). No eulogies are read, although the preacher may say a few words about the deceased, always in the context of the struggle now over and about the afterlife in paradise. The sermon—and it is a sermon—is also a traditional one, written by Hutterite forebears. The preacher, if he is skilled in this, will stop often and put the sermon into context. At one funeral service I attended, the preacher spoke mostly in the vernacular Hutterish language. People later commented on this, saying how much more of the service they actually understood because of that. While a good deal of the service is uplifting, it is also a very somber experience, and mourners get reminded—admonished even—to live a righteous life in order to obtain salvation. After the service, the family members take a last look at the body, and amid tears and outbursts of emotion, the body is covered with a white cloth and the coffin closed. It is then carried to the colony cemetery for burial.

Then, there's the wait. Waiting for the return of Jesus Christ to reward all those who dedicated themselves in community. The afterlife is vividly portrayed in many Hutterite sermons and songs, giving people the contentment to lead humble and simple lives, apart from the mainstream world, where the devil is believed to be king. During their early history, separation from the world and living the Hutterite way often meant hardships, and even death. For Hutterites, communal living and absolute belief in Jesus Christ made the difference, as it does today for many.

Their faith, like all faiths, has a history. In the next section, I will give a brief history of the Hutterite people, starting from the very beginning moving right up to the present.

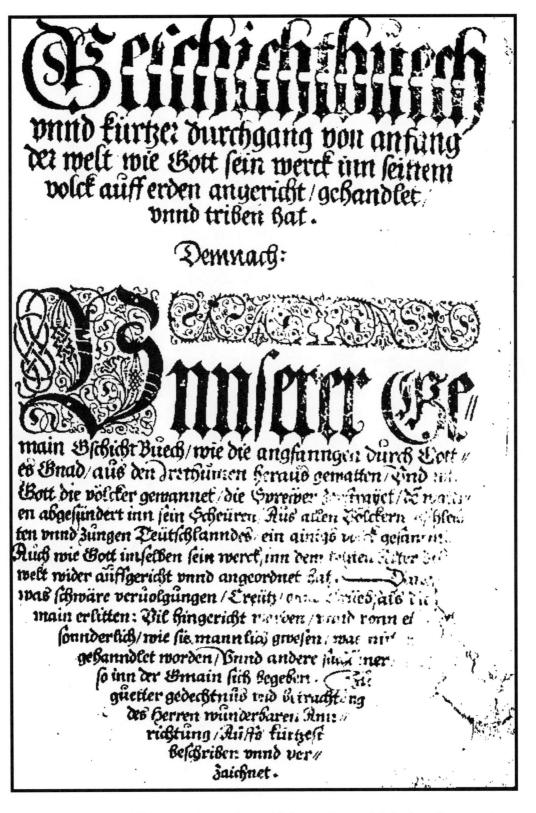

The title page of a 1581 Hutterite codex, which was first published as *Das grosze Geschichtbuch der Hutterischen Brüder* in 1923, then as *Die Älteste Chronik der Hutterischen Brüder* in 1943. The English translation *(The Chronicles of the Hutterian Brethren)* was first published in 1987 by Plough Publishing House, **Rifton, NY.** (Photograph—LA/TW)

Hutterite History

The Biblical Legacy

Hutterite history and religion may be likened to an oak tree, with the base of its trunk sitting on the Protestant Reformation of the 16th century. This is when Hutterite history, inasmuch as the Reformation affected its origins, began.

The Hutterites' spiritual roots, however, go deeper into the soil of time, through obscure centuries preceding the 16th century, until at last they reach the oasis of primitive Christianity as practiced in Apostolic times. It was then that the disciples of Jesus Christ received the Holy Spirit (today commemorated by Pentecost) and went out to preach the Word of God and baptize people. "And all who believed were together, and had all things common" (Acts 2:44). The chief religious tenets of the Hutterites are those of most evangelical churches—they believe in a personal God, that Jesus Christ was His only begotten Son, that he came into the world to save mankind through the shedding of His blood on the cross. What has distinguished them from other churches from the beginning—and still does today—is their practice and belief in the community of goods.

The Radical Reformation

In the first quarter of the 16th century, Martin Luther initiated the Protestant Reformation in Central Europe, one of the greatest revolutions of all times. It was a turning point in history, a stormy and often brutal conflict. Although it cut a wide swath into the hegemony of the Roman Catholic Church, the church and state alliance was carried forward by both the Protestant and Reformed churches. Some of Luther and Zwingli's closest supporters pressed for still greater reforms. Barely had these two groups broken away from the Catholic Church, when the Radical Reformation got underway in Switzerland (1525), quickly spreading throughout Europe. The radical reformers, so-called, argued with Zwingli that infant baptism had no biblical basis, that Christ's church as described in the Gospel of Luke was made up of voluntary believers: adults who requested baptism to signify their Christian faith. Moreover, this church wasn't run by a hierarchy of religious officials, many of whom worked hand in glove with the state.

Meanwhile, in the Germanys, and Switzerland, the Peasants' War of 1524-1525 was raging. After the breakdown of Feudalism at the end of the Middle Ages, a great many citizens had been left landless, perpetually at the mercy of oppressive nobles. The peasants, but also townsmen, artisans, educators, priests—even some nobles—wanted the Reformation to embody economic and political changes and bring about greater religious freedom. The rebellion failed, and Luther gave the thumbs-down critique to the peasants' attempted version of the Reformation.

Feudalism: *During the breakdown of the ancient Roman Empire, bold men acquired land, usually by military victory. These men, responsible to the king, granted parts of their holdings to other people (vassals, feudal tenants, servants, serfs, peasants), over whom they thereafter exercised certain rights, including taxation and administration of justice. Each small district was ruled by a duke, count, or other noble. The lords of a nation formed its nobility, their rank depending on the extent of their possessions. For at least two centuries before the Reformation, peasants had protested against serfdom and tithes; against restrictions on their rights to use the common fields, woods, streams, and meadows; and against their property owners' efforts to raise rents and increase labor services.*

Three of the so-called radical reformers who spearheaded the Anabaptist movement in Switzerland were Conrad Grebel (left), George Blaurock (centre), and Felix Manz (right). Felix Manz was the first Anabaptist Martyr. He was captured in 1525 and sentenced to death by drowning. His close friend, George Blaurock, fled to Tyrol where he preached, taught, and baptized in secret. He too was caught, then burnt at the stake in 1529. Jakob Hutter later guided many people from Blaurock's congregation to Moravia. (Photographs—Reprinted with permission from *Princes, Potentates, and Plain People,* by Reubon Goertz, Centre For Western Studies, Sioux Falls, SD)

Many peasants returned to the Catholic Church. Others joined the radical reformers, particularly the more visible group, the Anabaptists, labeled *wiedertäufer,* a derogatory term meaning "rebaptizers." Lutheranism mostly represented the upper social classes and princes, whereas Anabaptism represented the peasants and artisan classes. Driven by a tremendous religious fervor, they began baptizing each other upon confession of faith, and they denounced allegiance with the established church and state. Specifically reflective of Christ's teachings, the Anabaptists in Switzerland outlined in 1527 what is known as the Schleitheim Confession, which were guidelines for a simple, non-worldly lifestyle: nonviolence, forbidding the swearing of oaths (including civil ones), and forbidding service in the government, military, among others. From this gathering, distinct Anabaptist groups later emerged, such as the Amish, Mennonites, and the Hutterites.

Persecution set in almost immediately in Switzerland and the Hapsburg lands. Secular and ecclesiastical leaders were struck with panic by the potential of the movement, and set out to destroy it. The reforms preached by the Anabaptists were extremely threatening to the established social order. The persecution was ruthless. Believers were imprisoned, tortured, and executed. People from all over Switzerland, South Germany, Tyrol, Schleswig, and Upper Austria fled to the far reaches of the Holy Roman Empire, particularly Moravia (today part of the Czech Republic). Religious differences had been somewhat ironed out a full century earlier in Moravia and Bohemia, during the Hussite Wars (1419-1436), resulting in a tolerance still unknown in the Germanys. Bohemia and Moravia had just (in 1526) formed a

Holy Roman Empire: *An amorphous political institution of Western Europe originated by Pope Leo III in 800 AD. In its early stages it was called the Empire of the West. It was neither holy, Roman nor an empire in the true sense. Any holiness it attached to itself came from the claims of the popes in their attempts to assert religious control in Europe. Although the Empire played a considerable role in central European politics and ecclesiastical affairs, at no time was there a single government, a common system of law, a unified language, or a sense of common loyalty among the states within the Empire. It was dissolved in 1806 by Francis II, the last of the emperors.*

kingdom within the Holy Roman Empire, but at the death of King Louis II, this kingdom—including Hungary—came under direct Hapsburg control. However, because these lands sat on the fringes of the Hapsburgs, the nobles still enjoyed a considerable independence. It is understandable that they would be willing to grant asylum to the German and Swiss Anabaptists, since they stood to benefit from the German people's industrial success and agricultural production as they had for centuries whenever German immigrants had spread into Bohemia. Many of the Anabaptists, however, stayed in their homeland, continuing to practice their faith secretly.

The Beginning of a Communal People

In 1528, a group of about 200 Austrian Anabaptists living in Moravia on the estates of the Liechtensteins—which included Nickolsburg, where the largest concentration of Anabaptists resided—broke away from the main group. Led by Jakob Wiedemann, they held strictly to nonviolence, and refused to pay war taxes, whereas others advocated moderation in the avoidance of the world, bearing of arms, and payments of taxes in order that the government could protect its citizens. After the failure of the Peasants' War, these people had decided that a true theocratic Christian community was not possible under the existing political order.

On the way to Austerlitz, they stopped at a deserted village named Bogenitz, where a memorable event took place. Following the example of the apostolic community in Jerusalem, the leaders placed a cloak on the ground and everyone laid his or her personal possessions on it. Overseers were then chosen to manage the goods, which were given to the members as the need arose. The group settled at Austerlitz, on the estates of Lord Von Ulrich Kaunitz, a supporter of the Reformation.

Jakob Hutter

It was by no means clear sailing from there, because communal life proved to be very challenging, particularly as more refugees arrived. A man named Jakob Hutter, elected the leader of a group of Anabaptists in Tyrol due to his leadership abilities and missionary zeal, was sent by his congregation to establish contact with the communal group. This congregation also had strong leanings toward communal life, and soon more people, fleeing persecution, made their way to Austerlitz under the guidance of Jakob Hutter. His leadership and organizational skills were soon recognized at Austerlitz, too; and although there were people there who opposed him for selfish reasons, he was elected *vorsteher* (head preacher) of the communities in 1533. His tenure was short, though. He was captured on his way to Tyrol in 1536 and publicly burnt at the stake at Innsbruck. His communities became known as the Hutterian Brethren.

The Hutterites in Moravia and Hungary

In Moravia, the Hutterites went through bad and good periods. After Hutter, the persecution continued, directed primarily toward their missionaries, of which approximately four-fifths were martyred. The communities continued to grow in spite of that, because they gained many

---

Jakob Hutter: *This man was born and raised in Moos, near Bruneck in the Puster Valley of South Tyrol, which is today part of Italy. After receiving a scant education at Bruneck he went to Prags in Tyrol to learn his trade of hatmaking, hence the German name Hutter (Hatter). Footnotes in the Hutterian Chronicles suggest that he was a supporter of Michael Gaismair, the leader of the Peasant's Revolt in Tyrol. It appears that Hutter gathered around him some of the surviving partisans after the failure of Gaismair's armed uprising, and joined Anabaptist groups led by George Blaurock, "accepting baptism, true surrender and going the way of Jesus."*

converts. They had a particularly difficult period beginning in 1546. Because of the revolt and excesses of the Münster Anabaptists, King Ferdinand of Austria demanded the expulsion of Hutterites from Moravia. The demand was so persistent that nobles dared not refuse his orders, although they did so most unwillingly. The Hutterites were unconditionally faithful and conscientious in their stewardship over the land, fields, and meadows belonging to their noble lords. The nobles could not protect them, so the Hutterites were forced to flee and form small groups, hiding out in the mountains and making their homes in caves, which were elaborate excavations with winding passages containing trap-holes, living quarters, and hidden exits.

Conditions improved around 1551-1552 and Hutterites returned to their communities. By then, twelve *Bruderhofs* (Place of the Brethren) had also been established in Upper Hungary. The first Hutterite community in Hungary was established in 1546 at Sabatisch near the border across from Moravia. Plagued by persecution, many moved back and forth between the boundaries of Moravia and Hungary.

Then came the good years (1554-1565), followed by the golden years (1565-1592). Germanic islands set in predominantly Slavic areas, the Hutterite communities contributed tremendously to the economic development of southern Moravia. Feudal nobles challenged the Hapsburg imperial order and provided protection for the Hutterites, whom they considered excellent tenants. Hutterites flourished in many enterprises: agriculture, milling, managing large herds of cattle and fine breeds of horses, weaving, building, furniture-making, brewing, bookbinding, rope-making, pottery-making, and tool-making, among others. However, they refused to make war tools such as swords and spears. They were also sought out for their healing arts; Hutterite doctors were

---

The Münster Anabaptists *were prone to fanaticism. Laying aside the Anabaptist doctrine of nonresistance, they defended themselves by arms. They took over the city of Münster, which became the scene of licentious practices, until several Protestant princes banded together to defeat them, taking over the city and executing their leaders. The Hutterites had nothing at all to do with this, considering these Anabaptists to be corrupt and evil people.*

frequently called to the palaces of the nobility. By the end of the golden period, there were approximately one hundred Bruderhofs in Moravia and Hungary, with populations of well over 20,000, possibly as many as 30,000.

Early Hutterite Missionaries and Notable Leaders

Throughout good and bad times, Hutterites continued their missionary work, and were some of the most aggressive missionaries of the times. They wrote many songs, letters, and epistles, many of which are still in use among the Hutterites of today. The missionaries carried a pocket book, in which they proactively recorded their experiences and reflections, giving interpretations of the Bible, emphasizing communal living, thus shaping their doctrine. Much of this literature was produced while imprisoned—to send back to their congregations. The songs were sung to encourage themselves and their fellow prisoners. Adverse to publicity, the communities had practically nothing printed. And they hardly read anything but the Bible and their home-produced literature.

Peter Riedemann

Whereas Jacob Hutter had established order, Peter Riedemann helped the communities evolve further along the lines of more practical patterns of living. He also provided for the Hutterites a sound doctrinal basis.

After Jakob Hutter's death, one of his assistants, Hans Amon, was the *vorsteher* (leader or bishop) of the Hutterite church for a short time, followed by Riedemann, a Silesian shoemaker born in 1506. Riedemann was imprisoned numerous times for his Anabaptist faith. In 1540, while imprisoned in a castle at Wolkersdorf in Hesse, he wrote his *Rechenshaft* (Confession of Faith), which was written to express the fundamental elements of faith that governed the Hutterian Church to the ruler, Philip of Hesse. It is an exhaustive defense of Hutterite practices, supported by nearly 1,800 biblical references. One of the few Hutterite books to be published, it became well known throughout Europe. This definitive statement regarding such subjects as prayer, singing, baptism, The Lord's Supper, Christians and war, even dress and adornment, proved to be a flawless treatise on Hutterite beliefs, so much so that it has been adopted by Hutterites through the centuries. Some Hutterites called him the second founder of the Hutterites. He died in 1556, during the period known as the good years.

Ulrich Stadler

Stadler was one of the strongest personalities among the first generation of Anabaptists. Some of his numerous writings touched on the following tenets that helped shape the Hutterite church: Original Sin, Inner and Outer World, The Church of Community of Goods, The Functions of the Servant of the Lord (Bishop), Married Life, Church Discipline and Church Regulations. He died in 1540.

Peter Walpot

After Riedemann came another great leader, Peter Walpot (1521-1578), who is known for the organization of schools on the Bruderhof. He was the vorsteher of the Hutterian Brethren during the golden years in Moravia. As a boy of eight, Peter Walpot had witnessed the execution (burning at the stake) of George Blaurock, one of the men who spearheaded the Anabaptist movement. Walpot, a cloth-shearer by trade, headed the Hutterite fellowships beginning in 1565, which was also the beginning of the golden years. He was an outstanding leader, a well-read and creative writer and organizer who did much to bring the brotherhood to the spiritual and moral height which attracted many converts during the second half of the 16th century. He and his wife were also active (in 1546) in Silesia as missionaries among the Gabrielites, another small group who had lived communally in Moravia. During the 1570s, he drew up a catechism for children in the Hutterite communities (which is still in use today), as well as several prayers and hymns for children, to be taught in school.

Neumühl (Nové Mlýny), northeast of Nickolsburg (Mikulov), was established in 1558 and was an impressive site. At first there was only a mill there, belonging to the lords von Liechtenstein, who leased it to the Hutterites. The mill was rebuilt, hence the name "Neumühl" (New Mill).
(Photograph—LG)

Peter Walpot was instrumental in making Neumühl the political and cultural center of Hutterite activity. Here were located the archives, library, and communication center of the Hutterites. As missionaries went out, epistles were constantly arriving, then being sent out to the other communities. Hutterites were often the messengers themselves, making dangerous trips from their home base to imprisoned missionaries hundreds of miles away in Austria, Germany, and Switzerland. Also produced at Neumühl were medical supplies for the communities and other people. The village had a large distillery and cellar where the distilled pharmaceutical supplies were stored. Other enterprises included ironworks, wagon-making, and crafts. Their famous pottery was in great demand among Moravian lords.

Kaspar Braitmichel

Braitmichel was also known as Kaspar Schneider, since he was by trade a tailor. He was the first Hutterite historian. During the Peter Walpot era, he began writing the official Hutterite church chronicles called *Das Geschicht Buch*. It was an elaborate summary of church history "from the beginning of the world." His chronicles run until 1542, after which he couldn't continue because of his failing eyesight and other physical frailties.

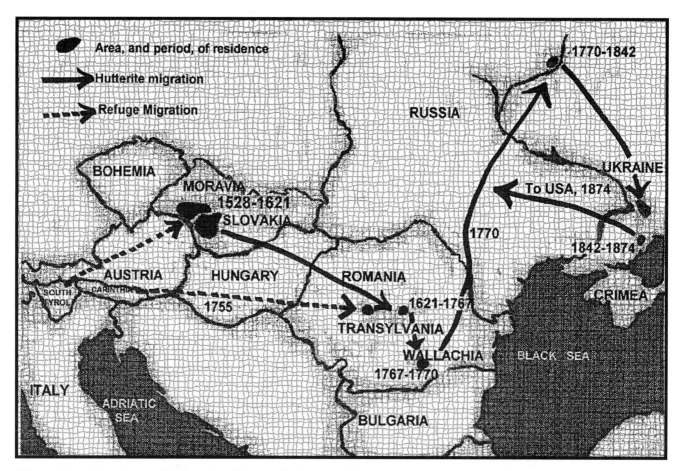

Hutterite migration and areas of residence, 1528-1874. The geographical regions of the 16th century are different from those of today. The regions of Austrian-Hungary where Hutterite Bruderhofs were located, is today part of the Slovak Republic. Bohemia and Moravia are part of the Czech Republic. (Illustration—SH)

Woodcut from the 16th century showing Hutterite dwelling and dress.
(Photograph from the title page of Erhard, 1589)

Hutterite dwellings at Grosschützen (Velké Leváre), in the present-day Slovak Republic.
(Photographs—LG)

The Turkish War and the Thirty Years' War

The golden period ended when war broke out between the Turks and the Holy Roman Empire in 1593. During the Turkish War, armies from both sides passed through Moravia. Because the Hutterites were pacifists and their communities very noticeable, they were easy targets. Other people suffered from the Turks' invasions and plundering, but Hutterites fared the worst. Because they had central food stores and community kitchens, soldiers could easily obtain food and shelter there, raiding the communities, killing people, and capturing many of the Hutterites, especially women. In the effort to fight the Turks, the nobles, who had provided safe havens for the Hutterites until then, were pressed by Emperor Rudolph II for taxes and war contributions. Many lords unwillingly complied and taxed the Bruderhofs. When the Hutterites refused to pay, sheep and cattle were taken, and large portions of the people's wages were kept as taxes for the war. During this war, sixteen Hutterite communities and eleven schools were destroyed by fire and eighty-seven members killed. Another 238 people were taken captive, most of them sold into slavery by the Turks.

During a lapse after the Turkish War, the Hutterites rebuilt their communities. They had scarcely recovered, however, when the Thirty Years' War (1618-1648) began. These were the most brutal years of all. This time it was the Catholics fighting a vicious war with the Protestants. The war was largely the ongoing Counter Reformation that had begun in the previous century as Catholics fought to reclaim the lands that had been lost to the Protestants since Luther's time. Now it exploded in full force in Moravia and Hungary. By now the Moravian government was mostly Protestant. It was a seesaw of battles, first Catholics gaining control, then Protestants, then Catholics again. When the Catholic armies gained control in 1619, the Hutterites were caught in the middle. Within two months, twelve communities were destroyed and seventeen were plundered savagely. Severe tortures were inflicted on the Hutterites. Many fled, taking refuge among their brethren in Hungary. Now the nobles, who had protected them before, could no longer do so. Twenty-seven Moravian lords were executed publicly.

In 1622, Cardinal Von Dietrichstein, a sworn enemy of the Hutterites, who had become the Governor of Moravia, expelled all Hutterites from Moravia. He gave them a period of four weeks, after which if they were not gone or converted to Catholicism, they would be killed.

The war took many Hutterites, but with it also came diseases, wiping out a third of their members in 1621. As the Catholic armies kept coming, most of the Hutterites fled, seeking refuge among their brethren in Upper Hungary. Some moved to Transylvania (today part of Romania). Their history will be continued later. In Moravia there were still a number of Moravian nobles who attempted to re-establish the Hutterites on their estates; but the Catholic invasion was so severe, they were crushed.

Although the Hutterites in Moravia fled to Hungary and joined their brethren there, the war caught up with them in this country when large numbers of troops moved in. So severe was the plundering and raiding in Hungary that by 1631 there were only one thousand Hutterites left in the country. Migrations, persecution, and loss of strong spiritual leadership had taken its toll. Other refugees and local people whose lives had been torn had no choice but to join them, not for religious reasons, but for economic motives. Many of these people, lacking the fervor of those who lived in community for spiritual reasons, drained the Hutterite communities' resources and even raided the colonies themselves. Hutterite chroniclers later attributed the decline of the communities to the many unfaithful people living within them at the time.

Andreas Ehrenpreis

There was a spiritual revival after this, during what is known as the Andreas Ehrenpreis era. A miller by occupation, Ehrenpreis was the first great leader born into the Hutterite community. He was elected vorsteher in 1639 and was in charge of all the Hutterite communities in Hungary. Through his influence and leadership starting in 1620, the Hutterite church evolved more toward a denominational type of church life, where things became more stabilized and regulated. It wasn't as dynamic as it had been a century earlier, but it still stayed puritanically strict. Mission and outreach were gradually fading, but the interior organization was well-disciplined and routinized. Ehrenpreis infused human warmth into the rigid Hutterite community, making the austere Hutterite life more practical and viable, a characteristic reflected in large measure in the Hutterite communities of today. Through his leadership, Hutterites were prolific in the writing of sermons, many with remarkable penmanship. The Hutterite sermons had to be "sharp" in contrast to the soft preaching of the State churches, where salvation by faith alone was enough. Throughout the Ehrenpreis era, 200 to 300 sermons were written. Among Ehrenpreis' vast numbers of regulations, epistles, and doctrinal tracts written to unify the Hutterites temporally and spiritually, his most recognized work is the *Sendbrief*, which he completed in 1652. This work was a courageous defense of the community of goods and an admonishment to his people concerning the tenets of communion, the highest commandment of brotherly love.

By 1660, the Hutterites had produced for themselves a tremendous wealth of literature. After that period, however, this proliferation stopped almost entirely, probably because the spiritual resources were exhausted. It was also coincidental with the decline of the communities. Although the fellowship had experienced a spiritual revival during his tenure, Ehrenpreis did live to see the decline of the communities in Hungary, which, as you can imagine, gave him much grievance and sadness.

The Decline of the Hutterite Church

Conditions got even worse for the Hutterite communities after Ehrenpreis' death in 1662. By now the Catholics had control of most of Hungary; they continued, the Jesuits in particular, to put pressure on the Hutterites to denounce their faith. Also called the Society of Jesus, the Jesuit order was founded by Ignatius of Loyola in 1539 and given its charter by Pope Paul III in 1540. Theirs was a potent teaching and missionary force. Loyola, drawing from his military background, gave the Jesuits an almost military structure. The Society had three grades of membership: priests, scholastics, and temporal coadjutors or brothers. Intensely trained in theology, philosophy, the art and sciences, and teaching, they proved to be an effective tool of the Counter Reformation in stemming the tide of Protestantism in Europe. Their zeal and effectiveness aroused fear and hostility not only outside the Catholic Church, but within as well. They were well known for their learning and political influence, and their "pious frauds."

Discouraged by the tortures inflicted on them, the Hutterites appealed to the Hungarian government in 1685 to consider them as individual householders from then on. Nevertheless, they continued to stand aloof from mainstream society, follow Hutterite traditions, practice the faith, and worship as congregations. These people became known as *Habaner*.

In 1688, the Hungarian government decreed that all children must be baptized. The refusal to do so was punishable by exile. Many Hutterites complied, permitting their children to be baptized by priests—"getting a bath," they called it. But the Hutterites rebaptized their children upon reaching adulthood.

From 1740 to 1780, the pressure was especially heavy. In 1759, the Jesuits petitioned Maria Theresa, Archduchess of Austria and Queen of Hungary and Bohemia, for permission to attack Hutterite fellowships and force them to accept the Catholic faith. Maria Theresa, being an arch-Catholic and a great friend of the clergy, gave the Jesuits full authorization. They were most effective. Fellowship in Hungary was reduced to four main centers: Sabatisch, Lewär, Trentschin, and Grosschützen. Not giving up, the Jesuits planned an attack on all four communities on the same day with the intent to rob the communities of all their precious books. They thought that without their history, sermons and confessions of faith, the Hutterites would soon give up their faith and convert to Catholicism. Fortunately, a sympathetic magistrate tipped off the Hutterites, and they hid their most precious books. The Jesuits hauled off many of the Hutterites' books and writings, some of which eventually found their way into State Archives in Europe. Other books were later recovered by the Hutterites, where the writings had been cleverly hidden in the walls of their homes and plastered over.

By 1763, most of the Hutterites in Hungary had converted to Catholicism. Persecution and spiritual decline had taken its toll. The Edict of Tolerance was issued in 1781, but by then there were no Hutterites left in Hungary.

The woodcut shown above is from the title page of a controversial volume published in 1608 by a Jesuit priest named Christoph A. Fischer. The book, titled "Fifty-Four Revolting Reasons Why the Rebaptizers Shouldn't Be Tolerated in the Land," apparently contained a wealth of information about the Hutterites of that era, but it also contained much malicious misinformation—the author's purpose was to discredit the Hutterites. Look closely at the cartoon and you will see what Fischer was trying to portray. Through the cartoon, Fischer compares the Hutterites' homes as pigeon houses, and Hutterites as pigeons, since pigeons live harmoniously and patiently among each other in small spaces. The cartoon also comments on some of the Hutterites' enterprises; they were tailors, shoemakers, stocking weavers, knife-makers, pottery makers, etc. The owl symbolizes the potter and the bats symbolize the astronomer and the alchemist, who work secretly by night. Alchemy is the Arabic Al Kímía (the secret art), so called not only because it was done in secret, but also because its main objectives were the three great secrets of science: the transmutation of baser metals into gold, the universal solvent, and the elixir of life. Through the symbolism associated here, the author was suggesting that Hutterites were involved in sorcery and witchcraft. The Hutterites (note the man holding the pot) were outstanding craftspeople. Their pottery enterprise was extremely successful. However, they guarded the secret recipes of producing colors for enameling their pottery. Fischer tried to suggest that this secrecy was part of the Hutterites' involvement with witchcraft. Note also the man with the long beard and open arms in the doorway of the pigeon house. This supposedly is Jakob Hutter. The illustration symbolizes the seductive power of the whole community. Propaganda was one of the Jesuits' myth-creating strategies—in this case hinting at the practice of witchcraft. Witches were burnt at the stake in the Middle Ages, and long after.

The Hutterites in the 16th century were solid and sober craftspeople and tillers of soil and vineyards. They also indulged in artistic pursuits. Their beautifully shaped and decorated enameled pottery especially received the admiration of many connoisseurs in Moravia. It was named after its places of origin, usually fayences or majolica. Noble families were eager to decorate their tables with the Täufergeshirr (Anabaptist pottery). The art had been dominated first by Italy, then by the Netherlands. How the Hutterites learned this trade remains a mystery, although all indications point to Italy, particularly because it is situated next to Tyrol, where many Hutterites were from. The potters were under strict regulations. Extreme care had to be taken with every detail, including materials and colors. Fancy, high quality pieces were not to be used in Hutterite homes, only sold to their customers. When the Hutterites were driven from Moravia in 1622, they took with them their pottery and the secrets of producing vibrant colors for enameling. The Hutterites who were forcibly taken to Transylvania by Bethlen Gabor's army in 1621 saw their art thrive there also. The princes of Rakocsi were very fond of the Hutterites' ceramics. The art continued to flourish after many of the Hutterites converted to Catholicism, although the sophisticated style of the 1600s slowly gave way to a more folksy style, more suited to Czech, Slovakian, and Magyar folk traditions. By 1840, the heavy competition with still more delicate bone china from Vienna had slowed down their pottery production and it was eventually phased out of the market. Today Habaner pottery, as it is known, is displayed in numerous museums in cities such as Budapest, Prague, Vienna, Berlin, Brno, and Bratislava. (Photograph—TW)

Although they chose Catholicism rather than fleeing to Transylvania (1725-1763) to preserve their beliefs, descendants of Hutterites in Hungary continued to live in large communal homes, and were called Haushaber (homeowners), which eventually was corrupted to Habaner. Apparently, the Catholic Church did not forbid communal institutions. Shown here (in 1965) are descendents of Hutterites at Sabatisch (Sobotiste), in the present-day Slovak Republic. These people were still living in homogenious congregations. (Photograph, 1965—MLA)

The slab of rock these people are standing on covers the Jesuit priest who converted their forebears to Catholicism. He asked to be buried there so that everyone who entered the building could step on him. (Photograph, 1965—MLA)

86

Hutterites in Transylvania

In 1621, at the beginning of the Thirty Years' War, when the Hutterites were expelled from Moravia, Bethlen Gabor, the Prince of Transylvania (which today is part of Romania), welcomed the Hutterites to settle in his country. He was a Protestant general in the war and favored the Protestant sects. But the Hutterites were cautious. They had been tricked before. When they wouldn't decide, Bethlen's messengers seized 186 people and brought them to Alwinz, near Hermannstadt, 500 miles from their homes in Moravia. Bethlen's offer proved to be legitimate, and the Hutterites were well-provided for there. Within two years 881 more Hutterites from Moravia joined them. As the Thirty Years' Wars continued, these Hutterites prospered while their brethren in Hungary suffered. Fortunately, they were able to send aid to their brethren in Hungary.

In 1658, war broke out between Turkey and the Hapsburgs. The Hutterites fled to a castle and the high ridges near their communities. After that, they never did recover from the Turkish raids. Frequently in these raids, the Hutterites' cattle were driven away, their villages plundered, the men carried off to the galleys, and the women sold into slavery. In 1665, Hutterite delegates from both Transylvania and Hungary visited the Netherlands to secure financial aid from the Mennonites. It was given.

But the Hutterites in Transylvania never regained their stability. Only about fifty people remained. The rest dwindled away, worn and discouraged by their history of raids, flights, and persecution. The Hutterites in Transylvania abandoned communal living entirely in 1690, although they too continued practicing the Hutterite religion. Their abandonment of communal living was almost parallel to that of the Hungarian communities, who abandoned it only five years earlier.

The New Hutterites

More than half a century went by. By 1755, there were only sixteen Hutterites left in Transylvania. The opening of the second chapter in Hutterite history initially had nothing to do with the Hutterites. Through the Counter-Reformation, the Catholic State had reclaimed Hapsburg domains, including Austria. However, in the 18th century, a Protestant revival began in the provinces of Carinthia, Salzburg, Styria, and Tyrol. More and more peasants were smuggling Lutheran Bibles into their homes and the country stirred with religious unrest. The Catholic clergy and Empress Maria Theresa were alarmed. In 1755 the Empress decreed that all religious dissidents were to be deported to Transylvania, located at the farthest corner of the Empire.

A group of Lutheran exiles from Carinthia, not allowed to purchase land because of their refusal to swear allegiance to the Empress, had to work out as laborers. The Lutheran church in Transylvania did not measure up to their concept of what a true Christian church was to be, so they found themselves estranged from their own church. Fortunately, they met the enfeebled Hutterites at Alwinz and found a great congeniality with them. Although the remaining Hutterites were not living communally, they were still loosely following their faith. After reading the old Hutterite literature and after many lively discussions with their brethren, the Carinthians accepted the Hutterite faith, subsequently congregating in two villages, Stein and Deutchkreuz. Here, under the guidance of the elders and the old systems of communal living, two new churches were established in 1762, thus reviving the Hutterite church.

To this day, the surnames Kleinsasser, Hofer, Waldner, Wurz, and Glanzer, form the core of communal Hutterite family names, and many people trace their roots to this Carinthian infusion. Surnames that can be traced even further back, to the old Hutterites, are: Mändel, Stahl, Tschetter, Walter, Wipf, and Wollman. There was a definite shift in the language and ethnicity of the Hutterites when the Carinthians joined the small group. Whereas the earlier Hutterites spoke a Tyrolean dialect, the new Hutterites' dialect overshadowed the old one, resulting in Hutterish (the Hutterite language) resembling more the dialect spoken by the Lutherans from Carinthia.

With more Hutterites around, they were once again visible. Persecution set in, forcing the people to identify themselves with one of the recognized churches, which were mainly Catholics, Lutherans, Calvinists and Unitarians. The Jesuits, too, were active. A Jesuit named Delphini was sent to Transylvania by Empress Maria Theresa to root out Anabaptism there and to force the Hutterites to attend Catholic services. With help from the police, Delphini went to work. The Hutterites were scattered into various districts. Many were imprisoned. With the fervor of the early Hutterites long gone, many of these people, including an elder named Mertl Roth, gave up their faith.

Hutterites in Wallachia

Two men, Joseph Kuhr and Johannes Stahl, whom nobody could convert from their Hutterite faith, were imprisoned for three years. Then they were taken to the Polish border and ordered never to return. Johannes Stahl had to leave his wife and four children, not knowing if he would ever see them again. The two men circled east of the Carpathian Mountains and wandered through Moldavia, then through Wallachia. In Wallachia, they discovered that people were free to follow any religion they wanted. The Wallachian people favoured the Greek Catholic religion; Greek, Jews, Armenians, and Phillipians lived in the marketplaces and cities. Although independent, both Wallachia and Moldavia were ruled by Turkish-appointed lords, who were usually members of Greek families from Constantinople.

The living conditions in Wallachia were ideal. The climate was warm and the land was fertile; bountiful grape crops grew here, and the pastures, meadows, and fields were lush. On one occasion, the two Hutterites met a lone shepherd. It appeared that he had no sheep. "If you are a shepherd, where are your sheep?" they asked him. He showed them where his sheep were grazing— in such deep grass that only their heads were showing.

With renewed spirits, the two men returned to their brethren in Transylvania, hoping to convince them to migrate to Wallachia. Their return was a relief to the Hutterites still there. Delphini was about to carry out a plan of attack on those who hadn't yet converted to Catholicism. Their children would be taken from them, placed into orphanages at Hermannstadt, and older people thrown into prison. If that didn't work, they would be banished from the country, as Joseph Kuhr and Johannes Stahl had been. The Hutterites decided that they would migrate to Wallachia. Because the authorities forbade emigration, they planned their escape in great secrecy. In 1767, sixty-seven people, including the sixteen members of the original Hutterites at Deutchkreuz, began their treacherous journey across the Transylvanian Alps, also known as the Carpathian Mountains.

They settled near Bucharest. During the first winter in Wallachia, they lived in crudely built homes, which were basically three-foot-deep holes in the ground, and lean-to's built from posts and beams overtop, which were then covered with straw and earth. At one of the gables, they made a doorway, and a window or two at the other. Although their homes looked strange, the people were satisfied. They had what they most wanted: peace and religious freedom.

In the spring, the Hutterite settlers purchased the land of a wealthy German friend named Wölfl, who had died during the winter. Soon their carpenters were busy constructing new homes. Others tilled the land, planted vineyards, and opened shops as weavers and potters. The local people were very intrigued by these industrious people and came to watch them work. To the Hutterites, it seemed as though they had finally found a place where they would be left alone, given freedom to worship in their own way, and be appreciated for who they were.

But scarcely had a year passed when war broke out between the Ottoman Empire and Russia. Historically, Wallachia and Moldavia had been an apple of discord between two powerful empires, Turkey and Russia. After 1750, Russian influence in these two principalities had become increasingly visible, and the Turks suspected Russia of harboring a scheme to overtake them entirely. Little did the Hutterites know that what they had accepted as a remote and peaceful principality (Wallachia) was about to be hit by another war, and once again they would fall victim to violence. Not only were they caught in the center of retreating and advancing armies, they were also caught in the path of roaming Albanian robber bands who had enlisted in the army under the pretense of driving out the Turks. The Albanian mercenaries prowled the country, robbing and plundering, especially the rich nobility. The Hutterites were also attacked, their homes searched for money, many of their members burned and beaten.

Hutterites in the Ukraine

By 1770, after having been in Wallachia for only three years, the Hutterites again decided to migrate to a safer home, this time north, to Russia. Under its young ruler, Catherine the Great, Russia was organizing the area north of the Black Sea into a new expanded territory. Seven years earlier, Catherine had released her famous Manifesto; the imperial government was striving to attract foreigners to settle in the Ukraine by offering them land under very attractive conditions. The expectations were that these colonists on the Russian Steppes would serve as models for the native population in farming techniques. The settlers were offered virgin lands, tax concessions, and other privileges, including complete religious freedom. Many thousands of Germans from the Palatine, as well as other foreigners, had already settled in the Ukraine.

Following the advice of Sämetin, a Russian general stationed in Bucharest, sixty Hutterites made the journey to Khotin, a city on the Polish-Russian border. There, Count Peter Alexandrovich Rumiantsev provided for them protection and the means to make the journey safely to the Ukraine.

Count Rumiantsev invited the Hutterites to settle on his estate north of Kiev, giving them a written pledge that offered not only religious freedom and freedom to live communally, but also exemption from military service and the swearing of oaths. Furthermore, they would have a three-year period of tax-exemption and would be allowed to retain the income from the sale of their home industries. As outlined in the Manifesto, they were also given an advance payment in flour and lumber, so they could begin to build their communities. The Hutterites accepted this deal and settled at Vishenka (in the province of Tchernigov) on the Desna River, 120 miles northeast of Kiev. There they built a water mill, a windmill, a school, and an ice cellar, planted a large orchard, and grew rye and winter wheat. Their community also thrived on enterprises such as weaving, pottery-making, metalworking, a distillery, and others. Count Rumiantsev was very proud of the work the Hutterites had done, and Vishenka became his showplace where he sometimes took guests and foreign diplomats.

After getting settled, delegates made several journeys (between 1771 and 1795) to Wallachia and Transylvania to visit the Hutterites in prison and to attempt to bring back members who had joined the other churches. Some journeys were successful, others were not. The representatives also traveled to Hungary and managed to persuade former Hutterites to join the Vishenka community. Also, on their journey to Hungary, the delegates met with Mennonites living in Poland and Prussia. From these, fifteen persons joined them, with surnames such as Entz, Decker, Gross and Knels. Except Knels, these are among the surnames in Hutterite communities today. In total, fifty-six people were brought to Vishenka.

Johannes Waldner

A notable Hutterite leader in the Ukraine was Johannes Waldner (1749-1824). He was born in Carinthia of Lutheran parents who were exiled from their homeland in 1755, and who had joined the Hutterite church in Transylvania. His recollection, *Denkwürdigkeiten,* is a continuation of the old Hutterite chronicles, and was the beginning of the second Hutterite Chronicle book known as *Das Klein Geschichtbuch* (The Small Chronicles). It wasn't actually printed until much later—in 1947. Johannes Waldner wrote the Hutterite story up to 1802, and the remainder was written by other historical Hutterite writers. What is interesting about Waldner was that part of his account (in

Transylvania, Wallachia, and the Vishenka community) was autobiographical; this helps the events he narrated come alive. Waldner was instrumental in reviving the old and genuine spirit the Hutterites had known during the Andreas Ehrenpreis era in Hungary before the decline of the communities and the abandonment of the community of goods. In the early years in the Ukraine, he spearheaded the collection and rewriting of old sermons that had been forgotten. Some of these writings were taken from old sermon notebooks. The Hutterites needed a rejuvenator like Waldner in the early years in the Ukraine; strong leadership was crucial after the people settled in a new country again. He was elected preacher at Vishenka in 1782, then vorsteher (bishop) six years later. He died in 1824, at the age of seventy-five.

The early years in the Ukraine were very peaceful for the Hutterites, although not easy, because pioneer years universally brought challenges. Throughout most of the Russian sojourn (1770-1874) the Hutterites were very isolated; not one marriage took place between a Hutterite and a Ukrainian. One of the stipulations in Catherine the Great's Manifesto forbade foreign settlers to proselytize among members of the Orthodox faith. In the very early years (in Moravia) the Hutterites' membership grew in large part because converts joined them in response to aggressive missionary work. But now they had no new converts other than fifty-six people from Hungary, Transylvania, and Wallachia.

In the thirty-two years at Vishenka, 172 Hutterites died. Through hard work and determination, however, the community continued to thrive materially. Spiritually, beginning with the leadership of Joseph Kuhr (elder from 1779 to 1794), then Johannes Waldner, there was a general resettling into the institutionalized community and the disciplines of the "old brethren" of the Andreas Ehrenpreis era.

After Count Rumiantsev died in 1796, things changed. His sons, who spent most of their time in Moscow and St. Petersburg, attempted to take away the special status their father had given his Hutterite tenants, reducing them to the position of their regular serfs. The Hutterites were

alarmed and sent a delegation to Czar Paul I, who had succeeded Catherine the Great. They were assured that their agreement with the Senior Rumiantsev was valid. But they were also made aware that in the future they would have the same legal status as the Mennonite colonists, which meant they would be allowed to move off Rumiantsev's lands and onto crown lands. At this time the Mennonite emigration from Prussia—which began in 1789, nineteen years after the Hutterites migrated—was about to resume and thousands more were to settle on the Russian Steppes.

In May of 1802, the Hutterites (about 200 persons) left Vishenka and moved to crown lands at Radichev, eight miles from Vishenka. By November, they had erected nineteen buildings there. They immediately continued most of the enterprises they had established at Vishenka, but also planted several thousand mulberry trees, adding silk-production to their enterprises.

Despite promising early years at Radichev, soon difficult times came again and the Hutterite economy ground to a gradual standstill. This time the decline was not from persecution nor war, but was due to internal conflicts. The community had too little arable land for their growing population, and since there was no land nearby, the leaders refused to branch out and establish a daughter colony. They feared that if too many miles separated the new community, the surrounding indigenous population would soon swallow the communities in the same way they had seen happen with the Herrnhuter Sarepta Brethren, another communal group that had come from Moravia and with whom they were in contact. The Herrnhuter communities, although successful in gaining converts, were too small and eventually assimilated into the larger mainstream society around them.

But there was also another reason, likely brought about by the overcrowded communities. Not only was there economical decline but also spiritual decline. During peaceful times, young people, wanting more individuality, lost touch with the old ways and the communal life of the elders. They began expressing distrust in their historic faith and subsequently became victims of their very own distrust, causing the slow erosion of the community life. Those who remained steadfast experienced great difficulties; often they were the older members, whose faith had been strengthened by persecution and suffering. However, as the older generation was passing away, the younger generation, lacking enough work and feeling isolated, lost touch with the real spirit of communal life. Gradually, the Hutterites' enterprises dwindled away and reached the stage of bankruptcy. By then, it was too late to branch out and start a new community.

With internal friction having accelerated, there was a split in the community, particularly between the elder Johannes Waldner and the apprentice preacher, Jakob Walter, who had come from the Hutterites in Hungary where community of goods had been abandoned. Waldner did not wish to give up communal living and the old practices and customs, whereas Walter wanted to abandon communal living. "I would rather die at the stake," Waldner said, "than to abandon the old ways." Unable to come to terms among themselves and in financial decline, the Hutterites appealed to the Ukrainian government for assistance. The government directed them to Johann Cornies, a leading Mennonite landowner about 350 miles south, at Chortitza. Cornies' plan was to relocate the Hutterites to one of the Mennonite settlements in southern Russia. The property was divided and Walter's group moved to Chortitza, under the condition that the Hutterites settle in Mennonite-style villages and as individual farmers.

But both groups experienced more difficulties. The Chortitza group found it hard settling in among the Mennonites. In 1819, Waldner's group at Radichev experienced a fire that ravaged many of their buildings, including houses, barns, and equipment. After that, Waldner consented to divide everything up. Hearing about the fire and of the community's abandonment of community living, the Hutterites at Chortitza were overcome with compassion, so they moved back to their former community. A new compromise was reached. The large buildings were used communally, but each family was allotted its own land and livestock. Twenty-four families moved and settled across the Desna River to a new community called Neudorf, while about the same number stayed at Radichev. Among those who moved to Neudorf was Johannes Waldner.

Although he no longer served as the official minister, he still held worship services in his own home. He died a few years later.

After the community of goods was abandoned in 1819, Hutterite life continued to deteriorate. For many people, private ownership brought suffering and hardships. It was extremely difficult to survive on the insufficient land individual families owned after dividing it among their members. People made their meager living in whatever ways they could: blacksmithing, weaving, pottery, and working in the forest felling trees and transporting them. Few of the people had a horse. Everything was done with oxen. Whereas the early Hutterites had considered education as one of the first priorities, many families now neglected education, and children grew up unable to read and write.

By 1834, after having lived in isolation for numerous years, the Hutterites had lost touch with the changing world, their young people had become illiterate, and their industrial skills had stagnated. In dire poverty, bordering on serious economic and spiritual ruin, they appealed to the government to move to new lands. Their requests were denied, so they turned to Johann Cornies for help. Cornies had a lot of influence with the government, and through his intervention in 1842, the entire Fellowship (sixty-nine families) was relocated 400 miles south, on the Molotchna river. Nearby lived a large population of Mennonites—some 6,000—who had migrated from Prussia and Holland as early as 1789. The area where the Hutterites settled was named Huttertal. Cornies was an influential agricultural and educational leader. He sent the young Hutterite men and women to Mennonite farms in order that they apprentice and acquaint themselves with modern farm operations. He also compelled them to model their communities in the pattern of the Mennonite villages, with homes on both sides of a wide street, and their orchards, barns, and fields extending back. Children—and adults too—were compelled to attend the village schools. The desire for learning was so great that an equal number of grownups and married people requested a teacher for evening classes.

Although the Hutterites dressed differently and spoke a different dialect (Carinthian), this interaction with other German-speaking people helped them get back on their feet. The intervention of Mennonites imprinted favorably upon the Hutterites.

I can imagine that the isolated life and the futile years at Radichev were like a sad dream when people reflected back. This lesson of the *hungersnot* (famine) particularly stands out in my mind, because it was mentioned quite frequently when I was growing up. Even today, this experience is held up as a reminder not to be wasteful, and to stay strong spiritually, because these are considered crucial factors in the success of a community. The lesson of not losing touch with modern farming practices imprinted in the Hutterites' collective psyche through this experience. It has resulted in a striving for ultra-efficiency and in keeping up with the times. Before migrating to the Ukraine, agriculture was only one of many Hutterite enterprises. In Russia, however, agriculture took the forefront because there were few markets and resources for craft production; making crafts was eventually discontinued. If the Hutterites were to survive in agriculture, they would have to keep abreast with modern technology. Another lesson learned was that of branching out at the opportune time. For a community to thrive and run smoothly, it must branch out when a certain population level is reached. Exhaustion of the workload and landholdings of an agriculturally-based economy generally results in stagnation and decline. The Hutterite ideal of success, very much alive today, is based upon a growth-orientated, capitalistic outlook.

While the Hutterites in the Ukraine now thrived economically, and continued worshipping separately from the Mennonites and electing their own preachers, some elders longed to return entirely to communal living. Inspired by the communally oriented sermons of forebears such as Jakob Hutter, Peter Riedemann, and Andreas Ehrenpreis, and having guilty consciences, they thirsted to return to the spirituality of the old days. They also feared total assimilation by the Mennonites. An elder, Michael Waldner, prone to visions and trances, was first admonished, then instructed by an angel to return to *gütergemeinshaft* (community of goods), giving the blacksmith-

preacher an analogy whereby the community of goods was compared to Noah's ark as described in the book of Genesis.

In 1859, forty years after their abandonment of communal living, the first group of Hutterites returned to communal living. Led by Michael Waldner, they eventually took the name Schmiedeleit (blacksmith people). A few years later, they moved from the large Mennonite-style Hutterite village called Hutterdorf to a village named Scheromet. Hutterites from another village, Johannesruh (named after Johann Cornies), joined them. Another group started living communally in 1860. These people became known as the Dariusleit, named after their leader, Darius Walter. The third communal group would form later, upon settling in America. They tried living communally in Russia, but weren't successful. These were the Lehrerleit. Their name also came from a leader, Jakob Wipf, who was a *lehrer* (teacher). In America, yet another name was given to the non-colony Hutterites who chose to settle on individual homesteads. Of the four Leit (peoples) these were the largest in number. They were referred to—even after joining Mennonite congregations in America—as the Prairieleit.

From the Russian Steppes to the American Prairie

By 1870, the political agendas of Russia had changed and the tolerant regime of Catherine the Great had given way to a more militaristic rule. Russia had become increasingly nationalistic, and in 1871 a decree was issued repealing the Manifestos of Catherine the Great and Alexander I. After a period of ten years' grace, the special privileges and status of German colonists would be terminated. Foreign settlers from the Baltic to the Black Sea were alarmed at the new decrees. Two laws were particularly troublesome: military conscription would be compulsory and Russian was now the required language of instruction in schools. To make matters worse, all schools were placed under the supervision of the state, the intent being to gradually assimilate all the subject races and the foreign colonists.

The Hutterites' and Mennonites' pacifist faith automatically made them conscientious objectors to military service, and their schools were regarded as one of the fundamental bastions of their faith. If they were to survive, emigration would be necessary.

In 1873, a group of twelve delegates, two of whom were Hutterites, left Russia and traveled to the United States and Canada to explore the

Hutterite delegates, Paul Tschetter (left) and Lorenz Tschetter (right). (Photograph reprinted with permission from the *History of the Hutterite Mennonites.*

possibilities of settlement there. The Hutterites traveled through Indiana, Minnesota, the Dakota Territory, and Manitoba. During this trip the delegates petitioned both the American and Canadian governments for exemption from military service and the right to operate their own schools. The Canadian government gave them assurance, but the American government, specifically President Grant, although he displayed an encouraging attitude, couldn't offer them full assurance, because these matters fell under the jurisdictions of individual states. At any rate, the delegates were sufficiently pleased with their findings in North America that they decided they should migrate there. The landscape of the American and Canadian Midwest, they found, was similar to theirs on the Steppes of Russia. In Russia, meanwhile, the government realized it was about to lose some 45,000 of its most productive

farmers. Representatives were sent to persuade the Mennonites and Hutterites to stay. They were promised, among other things, that instead of military service, they would be allowed to serve in alternative ways. Many people changed their minds, resulting in only 18,000 people leaving Russia at that time. But all the Hutterites,

The SS Hammonia. (Photograph—TW)

communal and otherwise, decided to emigrate.

They came to America in stages, between 1874 and 1879, after selling their communal and individual property to Mennonites and other Germans in the Ukraine. The first group of 113 communal Hutterites (who became known as the Schmiedeleit), under the leadership of Michael Waldner, traveled by railway from Alexandrovsk to Hamburg, Germany. There they were joined by an equal number of other communal Hutterites (who became known as the Dariusleit), under the leadership of Darius Walter. Other passengers included thirty-five to forty Hutterite families who in America took advantage of the Homestead Act of 1862 and settled in private ownership in the Freeman area of Dakota Territory. Also on this voyage were some 150 Mennonites and other passengers. They boarded the SS Hammonia and arrived at New York on July 5 after a stormy Atlantic crossing of sixteen days. From New York, they traveled by railway to Lincoln, Nebraska.

The land in the area didn't suit them, so they were stationed at Lincoln only for a little while. This is when an epidemic of dysentery

TOP: Communal house at Bon Homme Colony, South Dakota, built in 1875. (Photograph—TW)

BOTTOM: Bon Homme flour mill. The buildings at Bon Homme were constructed out of limestone, which was readily available along the Missouri River where the Hutterites settled. (Photograph—MLA)

In 1982, Bon Homme Colony was placed on the National Register of Historical Places. The Register honors significant historic and prehistoric sites in America.

struck Lincoln, and thirty-six Hutterite children and one old man died. To escape the epidemic, the Hutterites moved north to Yankton, in South Dakota. Shortly after, the Schmiedeleit found suitable land near Yankton and went on to establish the first Hutterite colony in America. They initially purchased 2,500 acres in Bon Homme County, naming their colony Bon Homme. The Dariusleit spent the first winter at Silver Lake, living in sod huts, but in 1875, they settled permanently at Wolf Creek, forty miles north of Bon Homme Colony. The two Leit had intended to form one colony upon settling in America, under one elder, but they were not able to reconcile their differences, and consequently settled in separate colonies. Still, in the early years, there were quite a few intermarriages between the Leit, including the Lehrerleit, who came later.

More non-communal Hutterites made the journey from Russia in the following years, until 1879, settling mostly in the Freeman area of South Dakota. The third group of the communal Hutterites arrived in 1877, led by Jakob Wipf, and

Buildings at extinct Milltown Colony.
(Photograph—TW)

were the Lehrerleit (Teacher's People). This group had attempted to live communally in Russia (1864) at Johannesruh, but without success. However, upon settling in America, they managed to establish a colony and live communally. They bought 5,440 acres and settled near Parkston, South Dakota, north of the Dariusleit colony. Their community was known as Elmspring Colony. After the last Hutterites had settled, the total number had come to 1,256, of which only about 425 settled in colonies. Of all the Hutterites

who lived in Russia, only two families are known to have stayed.

The Hutterites' arrival in America coincided with the opening of the American West to large-scale settlement. In the early years the world around the Hutterites paid little attention to them because there were so many other settlers. In turn, characteristic of the Hutterites to begin with, they took but a passive interest in the world around them, resulting in seclusion from the general population. During the early years in South Dakota, the Hutterites faced the same hardships that thousands of other pioneers endured. There were problems with prairie fires, grasshoppers, hail, marginal rainfall, winter blizzards, and spring floods. The boom to come in South Dakota was still a few years off. The Schmiedeleit and Dariusleit were indebted for several years because they had to borrow part of the money required to purchase their original land. In 1878, the Schmiedeleit established a second community, Tripp Colony, about thirty-six miles northwest of Bon Homme. The colony had financial difficulties and sought help from other communal groups, and it was given. These were the Amana colonies in Iowa and the Rappists (also known as Harmonists) in Pennsylvania. Not able to overcome their financial problems, however, the Schmiedeleit were compelled to sell Tripp Colony in 1884. The original record for Tripp Colony indicates that they sold the colony because of debts, lack of water, and lack of hay. These Hutterites settled very briefly at Tidioute, Pennsylvania, on land held by the Harmonists. But they failed to reach financial independence there also, so in 1886 moved back to South Dakota, establishing Milltown Colony.

Because of some colonies' financial difficulties, a few individuals also applied for claim lands, essentially leaving the colony to do so. A homesteader received 160 acres free. After living on the claim for five years, the settler gained clear title to the land. These Hutterites intended to give the land to the colony after receiving full ownership and go back to communal living. After five years, however, some homesteaders decided to keep the land and not rejoin the colony. This created ill feelings toward individual Hutterites, namely the Prairieleit (non-communal Hutterites) and served to further separate the Leit. Despite some colonies' struggles, most of them prospered and their numbers increased. By 1917, the Hutterite communities had grown to about 1,700 people living in seventeen colonies, including two in Montana.

Elias Walter

A notable Hutterite leader in the early years in North America was Dariusleit elder, Elias Walter (1862-1938). He was the son of Darius Walter. When the Dariusleit arrived in America, Walter was a lad of twelve. He later moved to Stand Off Colony near Fort Macleod, Alberta. What is most notable about this leader was his great dedication to the revival of the old, genuine Hutterite Spirit that had died during the Ukraine years. Through his efforts of gathering manuscripts and codices from every possible source, and making the Hutterite literature available in every Hutterite home, the movement received the "shot in the arm" it so desperately needed if it was to survive in North America. From the age of eighteen, Walter's gift for writing and publishing showed. He was married to Elizabeth Hofer in 1886, and had ten children, but continued to work tirelessly at his book distribution service. In 1888 he met John Horsch, a well-known Mennonite historian,

and formed a friendship that was very profitable to both men. A year later Walter discovered the original Hutterite Chronicles at a colony near Wolf Creek, which he hand-copied several times. Elias Walter was a bishop in the truest sense of the word; he was intensely concerned about the spiritual needs of all the Hutterite communities, not only the Dariusleit. He was a dedicated copier of Hutterite literature. In his lifetime he hand-copied innumerable volumes, including twenty-one sermon books, twelve epistle books, a commentary on *The Book of Revelations*, *The Article Book* (written by Peter Walpot), among others. He also collected hundreds of hymns and martyr ballads from various Hutterite codices from the 16th and 17th centuries, including those of Andreas Ehrenpreis. In 1914, his compilation of songs was published, the impressive 894-page *Die Lieder Der Hutterishen Brüder* (The Songs of the Hutterian Brethren). This was the first official hymnal of the Hutterites, and the first ever to be printed. In 1919, he published yet another songbook, the *Gesangbüchlein*. A bookbinder, Walter for many years bound all the sermon books of all the Hutterite preachers, as well as many copies of the Chronicles, hymnbooks, tracts, and other literature. When he passed away in 1938, one of his sons continued his work.

Jamesville Colony in South Dakota. (Photograph—MLA)

TOP: Schmiedeleit girls at Maxwell Colony near Scotland, South Dakota (1910). (Photograph MLA)
BOTTOM: Dariusleit at Wolf Creek Colony, South Dakota, with their steam Traction Engine.
(Photograph, 1925 or earlier—MLA)

Michael Waldner, a son of Schmiedeleit senior elder, Schmied Michel (Michael Waldner), from whom the Schmiedeleit got their name, with his grandson Paul—South Dakota (1918). (Photograph—TW)

World War I And After

Before the First World War, few people paid any attention to the Hutterite communities; for the most part, neighbors were on friendly terms with this peaceful people. However, when the United States entered the war against Germany in 1917, public opinion changed overnight, roaring through the towns and villages like a prairie tornado. Not wanting to support the war effort in any way, the Hutterites refused to buy war bonds (Liberty Bonds). Although they donated to the Red Cross and did relief work, few of their American neighbors thought this was enough. Because the Hutterites were German-speaking, dressed outlandishly, and objected to military service, they were treated as enemy aliens and were even thought to be Russian Bolsheviks. In Europe, they had been persecuted because of the prevailing religious intolerance, but in America the persecution was primarily due to the nationalistic and patriotic character of the Americans. The Hutterites weren't the only ones affected in this way by the hysteria of the war. The Quakers, Mennonites, and other pacifists also experienced public disapproval and outright hostility.

Some of the worst offenses were directed against the Hutterites. Like their forebears' communities in Moravia, which were always easy prey for the plundering Turks, the compact Hutterite communities were more recognizable by their neighbors. This made them more vulnerable.

A mob of overzealous, local patriots, caught up in the frenzy of the war, stole 200 steers and about 1,000 sheep belonging to Hutterite communities, selling them for less than half their worth at an auction. This was applauded by a county newspaper. A portion of the money was given to the War Loan Committee. Some of it was kept by the bandits. Vicious rumors were spread about the colonies. Bon Homme Colony had a decent milling enterprise, grinding flour for themselves and their neighbors. Now the rumor circulated that the colony minister, who was also the miller, was performing acts of sabotage by grinding glass into the flour. An FBI report later confirmed that it was not true. Glass had been planted there by overzealous neighbors.

After the Selective Services Act was passed in 1917, all men between the ages of twenty-one and thirty-one were required to join military service. The Hutterites had collectively agreed that their young men would register and report for physical examination, but that would be all. The men were not to wear the military uniform nor obey any military work orders. Brought before the military court, the Hutterite men, who were not as educated as the intellectual pacifists, were classified as stubborn and obstinate peasant farmers by the officials in charge. An actual transcript of one inquiry I read clearly reveals how little world knowledge and education these Hutterite men had. But they did remain steadfast in their faith and they followed their ministers' orders.

There were many cases of brutal torture inflicted upon Hutterite men who, once registered, were considered recruits. At places such as Camp Funston (Kansas), Fort Lewis (Washington State), Fort Leavenworth (Kansas)—even the notorious military prison of Alcatraz near San Francisco— young Hutterite men were beaten, starved, held in solitary confinement, and hung by their feet above tanks of water until they almost choked to death. Some were even chased across fields by guards on motorcycles until they dropped from exhaustion.

The Hutterite elders sent a petition to U.S. President Woodrow Wilson, requesting that the government change its policies and provide some alternative for military service. Nothing resulted in this, so a delegation of Hutterite leaders, accompanied by John Horsch as mediator, traveled to Washington hoping to persuade government leaders to make changes. While there, they also explained to a government official that if the authorities remained adamant, the Hutterites would consider emigration. Previously, in 1898, the Dariusleit, led by Elias Walter, had established a colony near Dominion City in Manitoba at the beginning of the Spanish-American War. The plan was to have all men of military age immigrate to Canada, where they would be free from military service. The war was soon over, though, and the Dariusleit later found the land not to their liking, because it was constantly inundated with floods. Feeling stranded and lonely in Canada, and realizing that the other colonies would not join them, the Dariusleit returned to South Dakota in

Alcatraz. (Photograph—SH)

1905. Now, in 1917, they were again in contact with the Canadian government. Washington did nothing about the Hutterites' requests, so measures were undertaken to begin moving some of the people north into Canada, particularly the younger members, to escape further military persecution. On the Canadian prairies, the war had created a labor shortage, so the Canadian government, anxious for settlers on the prairies, was only too happy to offer them military exemption, religious freedom, and the right to have their own schools.

The most extreme of all the abuses in the military camps and prisons cost two Hutterite men their lives. In 1918, brothers Joseph, Michael, and David Hofer, and Jacob Wipf from Rockport Colony were summoned to the military camp at Fort Lewis, where they refused to put on military uniforms, perform their work orders, and march in formation. Consequently, they were court-martialed and sentenced to thirty-seven years in the notorious Alcatraz prison. The camp commander later reduced the sentence to twenty years. Chained together by hands and feet, they were taken by rail to California. At Alcatraz, too, they refused to put on the uniforms and were taken to the lower level and placed into solitary confinement. Their cells were dark and dirty and stank terribly. They had to sleep on wet cement, which was made even worse by the salt that seeped into the cells from the ocean. During the first four days in solitary confinement, they received no food and only a glass of water every twenty-four hours. And they spent the last thirty-six hours in the dungeon "strung up"—their hands manacled so high to the bars that their feet could barely touch the floor. By the fifth day, when they were released, the men were suffering from scurvy, and their bodies were covered with insect bites. Their arms were so swollen they would not fit into the sleeves of their jackets.

Regular beatings also took place. The Hutterite prisoners were allowed into the prison yard for only one hour every Sunday. After four months they were transferred to Fort Leavenworth, Kansas, and arrived in Leavenworth near midnight on a cold day late in November. Chained to each other's arms, the men were marched along the street from the railway station to the military prison. People gathered on the sides of streets to jeer, and military men poked them with bayonets. By the time they reached the prison, they were wet with sweat. In this condition, in the cold air, they had to change from their regular clothes into the prison dress. Until 1:00 a.m., they had to stand in the cold before they were admitted inside. By then they were stiff from the cold. Later they had to stand outside once more. By 5:00 in the morning, they were in such bad shape already that Joseph and Michael Hofer had to be taken to the hospital. Jakob Wipf sent a telegram to the Hofers' wives in South Dakota, and they left Rockport Colony immediately along with other relatives. Unfortunately, the railroad agent told them that the telegram had come from Fort Riley, which was also in Kansas. Consequently, they lost a whole day and when they finally reached Fort Leavenworth, the two Hofers could hardly speak anymore. Joseph died that night, and the military ordered that he could not be viewed anymore. Joseph's wife, Maria, however, pushed the guards aside, and pressed on through various doors, until she reached the Colonel, where she pleaded in tears to be allowed to see her husband once more. This was granted. But she had to endure the last horrible insult. She found his body lying in the casket, dressed in a military uniform, the uniform that he so steadfastly had refused to wear in order to remain faithful to his convictions.

Joseph Hofer's brother Michael died a few days later. The brothers' funerals were enormous; many people from the other colonies came to pay their respects. The two Hofer brothers were the last martyrs in Hutterite history. The total number who died for their faith in the Old Country was over 2,100.

The other two men, Jakob Wipf and David Hofer, after more abuses, were later released. David Hofer was released a day after the second brother's death, but Jakob Wipf was held until April 13 the following year.

All these problems, especially the atrocious treatment afforded the drafted young men and the harassment on the home-front, made it necessary,

---

as far as Hutterites were concerned, to explore the possibility of emigration. Canada had promised the

Paul Hofer (1899-1977), a younger brother of Joseph and Michael Hofer, the last Hutterite martyrs. He was the author's grandfather. (Photograph—SH)

freedoms so essential to them. While the agitation by excessively patriotic and fanatical neighbors increased, so did the hostility. By 1919, pressure groups managed, through a suit against the Hutterites in Beadle County, South Dakota, to introduce legislation that would economically cripple all the Hutterite communities. In short, the objective of this legislation, as ruled by Judge A.E. Taylor, was to completely dissolve the Hutterite colonies as corporations. Under this rule, each Hutterite Community would be required to dispose of all its property exceeding 50,000. The plan, as it was clearly stated, was to "absolutely exterminate" the Hutterites of South Dakota.

By the time the ruling was in place, there were only five colonies functioning in the United States: four in South Dakota and one in Montana. The others had already emigrated and established communities in Canada. In their haste, however, to beat the deadline of the ruling, most colonies had sold their property at a substantial financial loss.

Several years later, the remaining two Lehrerleit and one Dariusleit colony also finally let go and moved to Alberta. Virtually all the young men of military age had immigrated to Canada in 1918, leaving the older and already married men to take care of the remaining colonies. Because of the great distance between South Dakota and Alberta, the young women who had also stayed, now had trouble finding husbands. The decision was finally made to leave South Dakota for good and join the colonies in Alberta. The only Schmiedeleit community that remained in South Dakota was Bon Homme Colony, the oldest Hutterite colony in North America.

Hutterites in Canada

Canada was, and arguably still is, a more tolerant nation than America. But Canada, too, does not welcome strangers easily, wherever they happen to come from. This nation is far from being squeaky clean from prejudices and racism directed at minority groups and other immigrants, which is terribly ironic. Many Canadians are descendants of immigrants who were themselves looked upon with suspicion when they first came to this country.

Although there was a stir of resistance when the Hutterites first arrived in Canada, this opposition dissolved quickly. For the Hutterites, it was good timing. The war had brought about an acute shortage of labor-power on the prairies, and agriculture in the West was one of the most important elements of the Canadian war effort. People like the Hutterites, known to be excellent farmers, were considered most valuable for the Canadian economy.

The Schmiedeleit purchased land in the Elie district in Manitoba, and established six colonies: Bon Homme, Huron, James Valley, Maxwell, Milltown, and Rosedale. Today, this area still represents the core of Hutterite settlements in Manitoba. The Dariusleit purchased land in southwestern Alberta and established five colonies: East Cardston, Rosebud, Springvale, Standoff, and Wilson Siding. The Lehrerleit also settled in southwestern Alberta, establishing four colonies: Milford, New Elmspring, Old Elmspring, and Rockport.

In Alberta, there was immediate reaction from other people who had settled in that province. Telegrams and petitions were sent to government officials, objecting to the privileges granted to the Hutterites. War veterans spearheaded a move to oppose Hutterite immigration, and newspapers, even *The Canadian Methodist* and *The Presbyterian,* campaigned against "war-resisters like the Hutterites." This pressure was enough for the government to revoke the military exemption granted to the Hutterites in 1919 and prohibit further immigration of Hutterites into Canada. The opposition didn't last long, however. People soon realized that Hutterites had no political connection with Germany; many people even admired the colonies for their frugality and self-reliance. Because they were quiet and law-abiding citizens, the public, and subsequently the press, or vice versa, soon lost interest in the Hutterites.

Due to the hasty departure from South Dakota, selling their land for much less than its worth, the Hutterites had not been able to purchase sufficient land in Canada to avoid overcrowding. They needed immediately to purchase more land in order to establish daughter colonies. Between 1918 and 1929, four more colonies were founded in Manitoba and eleven more in Alberta. This rapid expansion created another stir. It coincided with a sizable proportion of Mennonites immigrating to the Canadian prairies in the 1920s. In southern Alberta, the Board of Trade protested that Hutterites and Mennonites were buying the best lands in the province. Together with the United Farmers of Alberta, it pressured the Federal Government to stop the immigration of Hutterites and to prevent further expansion. The Federal Government rejected these proposals. North American economies were declining after the war, and as the Great Depression hit, things got even worse.

In 1931, the wind lifted the topsoil on the prairies into great black clouds. In the following year came a plague of grasshoppers. These insects devoured almost everything in their path—even clothing and wooden tool handles. A year later, drought, hail, and frost joined the grasshoppers in acts of destruction. The grain market collapsed. Many individual farmers and merchants faced bankruptcy, leaving taxes unpaid. The government had to offer assistance, opening relief camps and soup kitchens.

Hutterites were also hit by the depression. Mary Wipf from Sioux Falls, South Dakota, remembers those lean hard years. She was a child then, living in the only Schmiedeleit Hutterite colony in Alberta, near the town of Alsask. Her community had branched out from Maxwell Colony, in Manitoba, in 1932. It was the first and last Schmiedeleit colony to settle in Alberta. Mary recalls that one of her community's main staples was Blackstrap molasses. They also regularly ate something as basic as *Schreckmues*, a pudding made mostly from flour and water. After several crop failures, the people at Alsask Colony eventually left Alberta and moved to South Dakota, settling at New Elmspring, adjacent to the Lehrerleit's Old Elm Colony, extinct since 1918, when the Hutterites had migrated en masse to Alberta. Other Hutterite communities suffered too, but because they had self-sufficient economies, the colonies in general didn't suffer as severely as the rest of Western Canada. The colonies' diversity also helped them survive during the Great Depression. They did not depend on grain alone. They had steers for beef and hides, hogs for pork and bacon, sheep for mutton and wool, cows for milk, chickens for eggs and meat, geese for feathers, and so on. The Hutterites needed no government relief, and were solvent enough to buy out farmers who could not meet their mortgage payments. To boot, they were able to pay their taxes. Through the course of the 1930s, the negative sentiments that people had about the Hutterites were completely reversed. Municipalities even considered the Hutterites assets, and local authorities made efforts to attract additional colonies.

Throughout the 1930s, each of the three Leit established seven new colonies in Manitoba and Alberta. Because of legislative changes in South Dakota, two Schmiedeleit colonies even moved back there, purchasing land that had been held by the Dariusleit and the Lehrerleit.

However, none of the Dariusleit and Lehrerleit, who had left South Dakota in 1918, moved back.

By 1940, Canada had fifty-two Hutterite communities. The colonies continued to thrive, and the Canadian public had no worries about them.

After moving to the Ukraine in 1770, Hutterites' economies were mostly agriculturally based. By the time they settled in America, virtually all other types of economic activities had been phased out. The only manufacturing they did was to make their own household furniture, baskets, and tools, some of which were very innovative and impressive. Theirs was now a completely agrarian society. The move to Canada only strengthened this tendency.

Before the 1930s, all the Hutterite colonies' farming was done with horses. In 1918, the Manitoba colonies had on average 2000-3000 acres per colony, whereas the Alberta colonies, due to drier conditions, averaged about 1000-2000 more acres per colony. Cattle ranching was more important there; much land was marginal and used only for pasture. (For the same reasons, a similar ratio of Hutterite land holdings is in effect today as well, with some colonies in Saskatchewan and Alberta owning up to 14,000 acres.) The main crops of all Hutterite communities in the 1920s and 1930s were wheat, oats, and barley. Some communities had as many as one hundred horses. Each boy fifteen years of age and older was assigned a team or two. Due to the numbers of horses required for large-scale grain farming, some colonies had a prosperous horse trade.

Between 1920 and 1950, the face of agriculture changed dramatically in North America. Before this period, horses were central to the lives of Hutterites for seeding, harvesting, and transportation, but it was becoming increasingly evident that tractors and trucks would replace horses. The complete phasing out of horsepower took more than three decades. First came steam, then gasoline, and finally diesel tractors. As late as 1966, when I was four years old, horses were still used for light chores such as pulling wagons and stoneboats at Springside Colony, Alberta. When my parents were growing up, however, farming and traveling with horses was still a way of life.

Hutterite colonies in Alberta were usually thirty to fifty miles apart, so traveling to another colony took a good part of a day by horse and buggy. In the winter, people traveled with sleighs or sleigh-cabooses. A caboose could carry four to six people. It had a small coal heater built into the center near the front seat. When traveling with sleighs, people wore heavy sheepskin coats and placed their feet into sheepskin sacks. Heated bricks placed into the sacks kept people's feet warm for several hours. After motor vehicles were introduced in the colonies, cabs were placed on the back of pickup trucks, which could seat about eight people. These cabs were also heated with coal-burning heaters. Larger cabs, made to fit onto three-ton trucks, held about twelve people but were not very comfortable. The passengers sitting near a cab's heater almost perished from the heat, while those passengers seated furthest away froze.

The carpenter was one of the busiest people in the community. With the help of the colony blacksmith, he manufactured grain wagons, chore wagons, buggies, spinning wheels, skein winders, furniture, kitchen tubs and troughs, washing machines, butter churns, wooden buckets, baby tubs, and sleighs, among other items. The blacksmith and carpenter shops were usually in the same building, which was one long structure with a small room in the middle of the two shops. This room contained a five-horsepower gasoline engine that drove a long shaft extending from one end of the building to the other. Long belts off the shaft drove the various machines in the shops. In the washhouse, where the women did the laundry, a similar setup ran all the washing machines and dryers. The washing machines were made of wood, a tumbling or rolling type of box. By today's standards, these machines were very crude, and doing laundry was a cumbersome task. Water used for washing clothes was first heated to the boiling point, then caustic soda or lye added. This was left to settle, and then skimmed off. A small cloth bag filled with homemade soap was also placed into the washing machine. Every spring, each colony made large batches of soap. The soap was made from lard and fat scraps, which were placed in a vat and cooked for several hours until rendered into a liquid with a consistency of thick gravy. Lye and borax were also added. The liquid

soap was poured into wooden boxes, left to harden, then cut into bricks or one-inch cubes. Each family was allotted a certain amount that lasted for one year. Many colonies still make soap today, mostly for washing clothes. The soap is ground into a powder and added to the wash like commercial laundry detergent.

When electricity was introduced to the rural areas, many Hutterite elders resisted it. It was big leap for them. Until then, people had used kerosene lamps to light their homes. Because of their isolationist attitude toward the world, Hutterite colonies were often the last in their area to install electricity or telephones. At first they hooked up electricity only to places where it was most beneficial, such as the barns. Electricity for the sake of comfort was frowned upon. The older generation thought it was a tool of the devil—they feared that adopting it might bring about the demise of the colonies. It didn't take long, however, for the Hutterites to realize the advantage electricity offered and how much potential it had. By the late 1940s, most of the colonies had also installed electricity in their houses. By then, powered and mechanized devices, providing the colonies great savings in labor, had also replaced most of the old horse-drawn implements. As combines arrived on farms, threshing machines were retired. Women no longer needed to help set up stooks during the harvest. Hutterite life would never be the same.

World War II and After

Friendly attitudes toward Hutterites changed into open hostility during and after World War II. More consideration was given this time to people who refused to join the military on religious grounds. Both America and Canada made better provisions for people like the Hutterites, Mennonites, Doukhobors and other religious pacifists, who were given conscientious objector status. This official status enabled them to serve the country during the war in alternative ways. Any money the Hutterites contributed to the war went for medical supplies. Altogether, in the United States and Canada, 276 Hutterites served in some type of public service work. Some

Hutterites opposed to even this kind of service went to prison instead. But not all young Hutterite men had the same outlook. Twenty-six men actually did join the armed forces of the two countries.

To people who opposed the Hutterites, alternative services such as planting trees in national parks, handling grain at elevators and working in lumber camps, mines, paper mills, and church camps, were hardly enough. The main issue was Hutterite land expansion. In Alberta, people lobbied the Social Credit Government to do something to stop more colonies from developing, and farmers protested against Hutterites in small-town Canadian Legion Halls. This pressure resulted in the Alberta government introducing an unfair prohibition on any land sales to "enemy aliens, Hutterites and Doukhobors" in 1942. This was called the Land Sales Prohibition Act. Doukhobors, whose numbers in Alberta at that time were very small, were more or less lumped in for the sake of appearance. The Hutterites felt the legislation was discriminatory, which it was. For one, it checked their expansion. Worse than that, while it didn't include any other church except the Doukhobors', or religious organization or congregation, it singled out the Hutterites, refusing to recognize them as a church. The discriminatory legislation was created primarily to halt Hutterite expansion.

After the war, the hostilities continued. The Alberta Farmer's Union appealed to legislators in 1947, intending to "remedy the Hutterite situation." One of the charges the farmers made was that while "Canadian boys were fighting and dying for the very existence of the country, the Hutterites had increased their wealth, and those coming back from the war could not compete with the colonies." They also argued that Hutterite children were deprived of culture and their right to live as free individuals. "What will become of our schools, hospitals, parks, playgrounds, swimming pools, rinks, and churches?" they asked. "What will happen to all these things that mark our modern civilization—if the Hutterites are permitted to continue their expansion?"

In 1947, new legislation was passed in Alberta, which was even more discriminatory than the earlier one. The Alberta government imposed the Communal Property Act, which limited

Hutterite land purchases to 6,400 acres at a time. A colony was forbidden to settle within forty miles (sixty-five kilometers) from any other colony. This law was further changed in 1960. The forty-mile clause was eliminated, but now all land sales to Hutterites had to be brought to a hearing before a communal property control board. The legislation also specified that when land came up for sale, it had to be made available to the public first for a period of ninety days before the Hutterites could buy it.

One can side with any group on some grounds. The contention that people returning from World War II could not compete with the Hutterites was blown out of proportion by agitators. The colonies' land holdings per capita were small compared to that of many individual farmers. In 1947, thirty-three colonies in Alberta had 167,800 acres of land, giving the Hutterites a per capita acreage of 41.06 acres of cultivated and pasture land. When you compare that to their neighbors' holdings of 300 to 400 acres per capita, you realize how discriminatory the legislation was. Truly, if the Hutterites were the problem, as those who opposed them claimed, this country would be a poor one indeed and not worth defending at any rate. Clearly, Hutterites were scapegoats. Did they deserve the outright hostility and the discriminatory legislation passed in 1947? In the late 1800s, the Liberal government of Sir Wilfred Laurier had adopted the Homestead Act, modeled after that of the United States, and began systematically recruiting immigrants from Germany and Eastern Europe. The Canadian government encouraged people to settle in block settlements by people of the same language and religion. But it was never a deliberate Hutterite policy to settle in block settlements. Their colonies were a hodge-podge of discrete units, some clustered, others more widely scattered. The farm population displaced by Hutterite colonies was usually minimal.

Even after the discriminatory legislation passed in 1947, the anti-Hutterite agitators still weren't satisfied. They demanded after 1956 that the colonies be forcibly dissolved. Some Hutterites in Alberta looked to Saskatchewan for expansion. The first colony was established at Shaunavon in 1949. In this province, too, opposition against them rose immediately. The provincial

Levi Tschetter from New Elm Spring Colony, South Dakota. During World War II (1943) he worked as an orderly at Staunton State Hospital in Staunton, Virginia. This type of work was approved by Hutterite elders. Later, going against Hutterite regulations, although he was still a conscientious objector, he served as a Forest Service smoke-jumper (shown in photograph) at Missoula, Montana. Several Hutterite men who started out serving in occupations assigned to conscientious objectors went against their elders' wishes and joined the military. They essentially had to leave the colony to do so, which meant they were outside the "ark" of community. After the war, however, some returned to colony life. Later, during the Vietnam and Korean Wars, Hutterites also left colonies—this time even more than before—to serve in the army. (Photograph, 1945—MW)

government studied the situation and concluded that the Hutterites were no threat to the province. As in Alberta, a liaison office was established in Saskatchewan to assist Hutterite settlements. Seven more colonies were established in the 1950s, mostly in the southwestern part of the province. Meanwhile, in Alberta, some colonies went out of their way to cultivate harmony. They offered free labor to help build community halls and ice rinks, which ironically, they never benefited from, because Hutterite children were forbidden by their elders to use these facilities.

Public and government attitudes toward Hutterites changed during the 1960s and 1970s. The Diefenbaker Government was instrumental in helping people become more aware of civil liberties, and attacks on minorities became less tolerated. Still, the Communal Property Act in Alberta persisted in various forms until 1973, when Peter Lougheed's Conservatives appointed a select committee to re-examine the "Hutterite Situation." It found that the provincial Community Property Act violated the federal Human Rights Act passed in 1966. The discriminatory legislation was abolished and all restrictions on Hutterite expansion and land purchases were wiped from the law books. For the first time in thirty years, the Hutterites were free to purchase land in Alberta however and wherever they wanted. Despite public protest, 44,475 acres were purchased by colonies within five months, and seven new colonies were established.

In Manitoba, there was also opposition to Hutterite expansion, but it took a different form. Similar laws to those in Alberta were discussed, but they never became law. Support from individuals and the Civil Liberties Union prevented any restrictive legislation; but pressure from the Union of Manitoba Municipalities did lead to a "Gentleman's Agreement" between the Hutterites and the municipalities in 1957, which was similar to the Communal Property Act of Alberta. The Hutterites consented that it was in their and the municipalities' best interest to establish no more than two colonies in a large municipality and only one colony in a small municipality. They also agreed to limit a colony's acreage to 5,120 acres, with colonies at least ten miles (sixteen kilometers)

apart. Twelve new Manitoba colonies were established in the 1950s, and another twelve in the 1960s.

Some Schmiedeleit colonies eventually moved back to South Dakota. In 1935, the South Dakota Legislature made changes that were favorable to the Hutterites. The government in that state passed the Communal Corporation Act, which granted the same tax privileges to communally-owned farms as were granted to corporations. Between 1936 and 1952 seven colonies in Manitoba moved back or branched out to South Dakota. Also, the one colony that had stayed in South Dakota (Bon Homme) branched out several times after 1918. After a series of expansions in South Dakota, however, the State Legislation in 1955 ceased to grant corporate privileges to the Hutterites. Existing colonies were prohibited from buying or leasing additional lands. But they continue to form colonies nevertheless. For the most part, the South Dakota legislature has avoided touching the issue, and courts haven't tested the 1955 Acts of Repeal. Since then, Schmiedeleit colonies have also been established in North Dakota (six) and Minnesota (six). The total number of colonies in South Dakota in 1998 is fifty-three.

Even before World War I, two colonies had been established in Montana. In 1918, when the Hutterites moved en masse to Canada, one colony of Dariusleit stayed in Montana. This was Spring Creek Colony, near Lewistown. But since they were outside the circle of Hutterite colonies, they were very isolated. When an offer came up to repopulate one of the colonies that had moved to Alberta, they moved back to South Dakota. This colony then split in 1924 and half of the people also moved to Alberta, settling near Lethbridge. Two years later, they moved from Lethbridge to Pincher Creek and established Pincher Creek Colony. By the mid-1950s, Pincher Creek Colony's population had reached its maximum capacity and, squeezed by the Communal Property Act, the elders looked for new lands to expand to. Somewhat of a maverick group, they considered moving to Mexico, and several elders went to Chihuahua, Mexico, to look at land supposedly owned by real estate agents in Vancouver, British

Columbia. When the real estate agency was found fraudulent it its dealings, the colony considered Saskatchewan, then Montana. Not being able to agree among each other whether to buy land in Saskatchewan or Montana, they finally purchased land in the State of Washington. In 1960, the first Dariusleit settled at Espanola Colony, west of Spokane. Today, there are five Dariusleit colonies in Washington. In Washington, there is also a small communal group (the Fan Lake Brethren) that was established in 1990 by a man named Don Murphy. Although Murphy is not an ethnic Hutterite, his group operates in accordance with the teachings and traditions of the Hutterite church. They own a small ranch of 180 acres, which supports a beef cattle operation and a commercial gardening enterprise. Their main occupation, however, is a computer-aided drafting company named Applied Computing Services.

Due to the Communal Property Act squeeze, other Dariusleit and Lehrerleit colonies looked to Montana for migration. The first two, one Dariusleit colony and one Lehrerleit colony, were established in that state in 1945. Others followed soon after. As of 1998, Montana was home to fourteen Dariusleit colonies and twenty-nine Lehrerleit colonies, not including those being built at this time. Except for some of the Washington colonies, the Hutterites in the United States are on average not as wealthy as the Canadian Hutterites. This is the case despite the Canadian dollar generally being lower in value than the American dollar. Consistently higher prices for agricultural commodities, in part due to Canadian quotas and marketing boards, have made the Canadian colonies wealthier than most of their American counterparts.

Paul Gross

One of the people who helped found Espanola Colony in the State of Washington in 1960 was Paul S. Gross. His leadership coincided with a period of rapid growth and changes in the Hutterite communities. In the span of his lifetime (1910-1998), the Hutterites grew from fifteen colonies to over 400, and Hutterites advanced from farming with horses to utilizing large tractors and computer technology. Just as importantly,

Hutterites emerged from being a neglected and misunderstood people to a frequently studied people.

Paul's flair for writing and intellectual matters showed at an early age, and while still living in South Dakota, he was given a high school education. His people intended to send him to college as well, but when they immigrated to Canada in 1924, his academic training was put on hold. Consequently, Paul never did attend college. The lack of higher education, however, did not impede his intellectual growth.

In 1949, by then already a German schoolteacher at Pincher Creek Colony, Alberta, Paul was elected to the ministry. Only a week after he had begun preaching, his uncle, the head preacher at Pincher Creek, died, leaving Paul to carry the full load of leading a community without having had the benefit of apprenticing for a few years. Paul himself didn't get an assistant till after six years of preaching.

Despite being isolated from other colonies after his community moved across the Rocky Mountains to the plateaus of Washington, Paul continued to influence Hutterites from other communities. His interest in the Hutterite way wasn't for scholarly purposes though. His main concern was to promote the Hutterian Brethren Church and what it stands for. He was a gifted leader and policy maker, a peacemaker among his people, an author and bookseller, a pamphleteer and publisher—he even fought against the atomic bomb! His best-known writing was his highly acclaimed book, *The Hutterite Way*, published in 1965. This was the first time a Hutterite had written a book in English. Since its publication, virtually all major Hutterite scholars have made it part of their research material. Paul himself benefited a lot from his relationships with archivists, historians and sociologists, including people like Karl A. Peter, Leonard Gross, and John Hostetler. His openness and willingness to educate others about Hutterite life and religion won him a lot of respect in the academic community at home and abroad. In his lifetime he collected a wealth of material from both North American and European archives, including letters, documents, articles, and sermons, some of which haven't even been transcribed yet. He understood the value in having an educated mind and was living proof that education need not weaken a traditonal society such as the Hutterites'.

In 1995, Vance Joseph Youmans, a curator of the Lincoln County Historical Museum in Washington and an Instructor of English as a Second Language at Eastern Washington University, published *The Plough and the Pen: Paul S. Gross and the Establishment of the Spokane Hutterian Brethren*. Not only is this an interesting book, it is also a highly important one. Since scholars typically write about the Hutterite communities as a whole, an individual colony's history is rare. The well-documented details in Youmans' book helps fill a missing link in Hutterite historiography, as well as give insight into what makes a notable Hutterite leader. This is just one of the many ways Paul Gross's work inspired people. Like Johannes Waldner and Elias Walter before him, Paul Gross will no doubt be a central figure in future chronicles of the Hutterite people. He died in April, 1998, at the age of eighty-eight.

The flooding of Standoff Colony near Fort Macleod, Alberta, due to heavy rains and the thawing of snow from the Rocky Mountains. Established in 1918, Standoff was one of the first Dariusleit colonies in Canada. (Photograph, 1964—CLA)

Hutterite playing harmonica—about 1950. (Photograph—JE/TW)

TOP: Deerfield Colony, Montana—established in 1947. (Photograph—JE/TW)
BOTTOM: Buck Ranch Colony, Alberta—around 1950. (Photograph—JE/TW)

Hutterite man around 1950. (Photograph—JE/TW)

Dariusleit woman and child at Kings Ranch Colony, Montana—early 1950s. (Photograph—JE/TW)

TOP: Dariusleit kindergarten children—mid 1940s to 1950. Note the absence of toys. Today, Hutterite children have many toys. (Photograph— JE/TW)

BOTTOM: Lehrerleit baby-sitter—mid 1940s to 1950. (Photograph— JE/TW)

Hutterite students—mid 1940s to 1950. (Photograph—JE/TW)

Monarch Colony near Lethbridge, Alberta. This Lehrerleit colony was established around 1942 by excommunicated members of Big Bend Colony, near Cardston, Alberta. In 1938, Jakob Mändel, the first preacher at Big Bend, was accused of having registered and then sold for $600 the patent of a rock gathering machine which he had constructed himself. This breach of community trust and bearing of "false witness" prompted the elders to remove him from office. Mändel, who believed he was acting in his community's interest, refused the order. He continued preaching to part of the colony, namely his relatives. This created a schism within the community. By 1942, Mändel was willing to split the community's property and to leave with his followers. The other party refused to grant the banned preacher his wish. He then sued Big Bend Colony and won, taking $30,000 from the colony's treasury, which he used to found Monarch Colony. Years later, faced with a dwindling population (marriages between cousins were already taking place), Monarch seniors begged Hutterite elders for reconciliation with the Hutterian Brethren Church. Their request for re-admittance into the church was turned down. At least two people later joined Dariusleit and Schmiedeleit colonies. Others joined the Holdeman Mennonites in Alberta. Only one family remains at Monarch today. (Photograph, early 1950s—JE/TW)

TOP: Hog barn manager—1940s. (Photograph—MLA)
BOTTOM: Preacher at Kings Ranch Colony in Montana halts the wheat harvest just long enough to tell the young men that he had heard rain was predicted (likely from the researcher who took this photograph, because the preacher would not have had a radio himself) and they should hurry—mid 1940s to 1950. (Photograph—JE/TW)

TOP LEFT: Car at Hutterite colony in South Dakota—1955. (Photograph—MLA)
TOP RIGHT: Haying season at Kings Ranch Colony, Montana—early 1950s. (Photograph—JE/TW)
BOTTOM: Applying liquid fertilizer to a wheat field at Espanola Colony, near Spokane, Washington.
(Photograph, early 1960s—LB/WH)

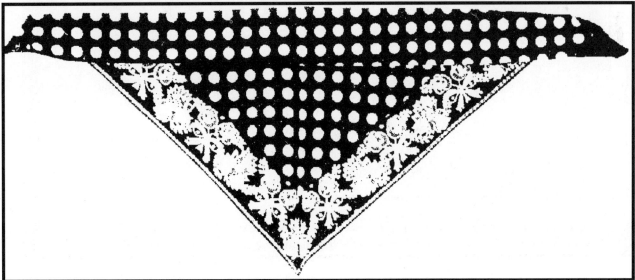

TOP: Young Dariusleit women—early 1960s. (Photograph—LB/WH)
BOTTOM: Lehrerleit girl's kerchief. Embroidered kerchiefs were popular among Lehrerleit women from the 1940s to the 1970s. The usual colors for the needlework designs were blue and white. Later, acrylic inks were used. To give kerchiefs the desired stiffness, Hutterite women soaked them in skim milk. Today, they use commercial fabric starch. (Photograph—SH)

Young Hutterite woman's fancy needlework, which was particularly popular during the 1930s and 1940s. The multicolored designs—the tree of life, hearts, stars, baskets of flowers, facing birds, and geometric figures—were all European motifs the Hutterites brought with them to North America. Working on towels like the one shown above was an exellent way to acquire needlework skills. (Photograph—SH)

In the 1950s and earlier, giving someone a friendship handkerchief was an excellent way to express love or affection. Hutterite girls gave them to boyfriends at Christmas, Easter, or birthdays. Some girls even made them for other girls as tokens of friendship. The needlework was very complicated and impressive. (Photograph—SH)

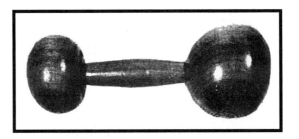

OPPOSITE PAGE:
Samples of Hutterite antiques: Spinning wheel, comb holder, red willow basket, sock darning tool, and *trugn* (wooden chest). (Top four photographs—SH) (Bottom photograph—LA/TW)

In the 1960s and 1970s, many Hutterites began selling artifacts such as these (usually the smaller items), often for much less than their worth. Because individuals received only two to four dollars allowance from the colony treasurer each month, collectors driving from colony to colony found many eager sellers looking to make some spare cash. Unlike moonlighting for private money, selling personal items for profit was not considered a sin. Many priceless antiques were lost. Fortunately though, the Glenbow Museum in Calgary, Alberta, was active in acquiring Hutterite artifacts, and now has an impressive collection of more than 2000 items. At least there they are safe in one place.

THIS PAGE:
TOP: The shlofbonk is a unique piece of Hutterite furniture. During the day it is a sturdy bench and at night it becomes a bed for children. The shlofbonk has not outlived its usefulness in many Hutterite homes, particularly in colonies where sofas are not allowed. A few Hutterite carpenters still manufacture the shlofbonk today. (Photograph—SH)
CENTRE: Hutterite casket. (Photograph—TW)
BOTTOM: Small stainless steel pails manufactured by Hutterite tinsmith. These pails are used for carrying food from the community kitchen to the house. The tinsmith also makes larger pails. (Photograph—SH)

TOP: **Hog barns at Rose Valley Colony, Saskatchewan.** (Photograph, 1996—SH)
BOTTOM: **Harvesting wheat at Rose Valley Colony, Saskatchewan.** (Photograph, 1997—SH)

Hutterites in a Changing World

By 1960, another stage of mechanization had reached the Hutterite colonies. Highly specialized labor-saving devices such as automatic milking machines and forage harvesters made more labor available in the direct production of agricultural commodities. After 1965, the push for everything modern accelerated in Hutterite colonies. Certain customs were modified or dropped. Natural gas and propane replaced coal, and house styles changed. Passenger vans and crewcabs were introduced. Three-ton trucks were replaced by large tandem trucks. Tractors such as the Massey Harris Challenger, Oliver 66, McCormick Farmall (Super M), and the Super W-6 McCormick-Deering International were now too small for the field. Generations saw the colonies move through increasingly larger tractors with more horsepower. Some of these were the 706 International and 1030 Case. Later they became bigger yet, when tractors such as the 4850 John Deere and various models of four-wheel-drive tractors arrived. These were able to pull larger and wider cultivators and seeders. Swathers and combines also grew in size, enabling colonies to harvest larger numbers of acres faster and more efficiently. No longer were the Hutterites the last to bring new technologies to their operations. Today they are often among the first. Innovative companies with new products often seek out the Hutterites to introduce to them the latest advances in technology.

In the barns, computers were introduced to carry out functions such as mixing feed, allotting rations to dairy cows and hogs, controlling ventilation for maximum efficiency, and record-keeping. The barns got bigger. Small 40-by-100-foot hog barns were outdated. Soon 60-by-200-foot barns became the norm, then mega barns, some up to six hundred feet long, running operations with 300, 600, even 800 sows. To keep the hog barns disease-free only the workers are allowed inside. Because there is no quota system for hogs, Hutterite colonies have capitalized on this market. Hogs have become one of the largest sources of income for most colonies. In 1991, the Hutterites in Manitoba supplied one-third of the

hogs in the province. I think back to 1966 and to Springside Colony in Alberta. I remember watching pigs move about in the creek behind the chicken barns. They were often fed kitchen slop. Today, a very expensive computer monitors and controls their diet, giving them the exact nutrition they need for optimum weight gain.

Before milking machines were installed, the women did the milking on a rotational basis. Then they were relieved of that duty. The milk was separated and the cream sold to local creameries. Colonies also had regular cream customers, who sometimes drove quite a few miles to obtain the unpasteurized cream. The skimmed milk was consumed by the people in the colony or used to make cheese. Any surplus was fed to the calves and hogs. When dairy quotas were introduced in Canada, Hutterites installed cooling tanks in their dairy barns to store the whole milk. Now the milk was routinely collected by dairy board trucks and hauled to processing plants in the cities. For most colonies, the dairy business was—as it is today—very profitable. The dairy enterprise provides "clean income," which means that the margins are good compared to other businesses. In Canada, the size of most colonies' dairy herd is sixty to eighty cows. But in the last fifteen years quotas have become harder to obtain. The quota system regulates the amount of milk that is produced for the market. Some colonies, at the time of branching out, have opted to split their quota with the daughter colony. A few colonies were not able to obtain milk quotas, and consequently milk only enough cows to supply milk for their own use.

In the chicken barns, eggs were first gathered by hand, using baskets. Then laying hens were housed in massive wire cages, and flat-bed carts holding tall stacks of egg cartons were pushed from one end of a barn to the other between rows of cages as the poultry workers collected the eggs. Finally, that too became outdated in most colonies, and the eggs are now automatically collected and delivered to the egg grading station via conveyor belts. For many years, colonies have also conducted a good business selling their chickens. On the evening of butchering day at Baildon Colony, our customers lined up for half-a-mile. Some people drove many miles to buy our grain-fed broiler chickens. The chickens were sold before the chicks were even hatched. In Saskatchewan and Alberta, colonies raise geese and ducks mostly for their own consumption and for the feathers. At Baildon, we hatched and raised about 1,200 geese every year. About half of them were sold to customers in Moose Jaw and neighboring towns. Of the 900 ducks we raised every year, we sold but a few. Serving cooked duck for the Wednesday or Sunday noon meal is practically a tradition in most colonies. Even the Cargill feed sales representative, who routinely came to sell more prepared feed to the stockmen at Baildon, knew that. He always came on Wednesday, conveniently a half-hour before dinner. In Manitoba, Hutterite colonies took over the entire goose market. By 1981, their market share had reached 300,000 geese per year, which was more than ninety-five percent of the market. Turkey production is also higher in Manitoba (about twenty percent of the Manitoba market in 1968) than in colonies further west. As with eggs, this market is controlled by quotas.

On the fields, crops and methods of farming changed as well. Like almost all farmers, Hutterites started using fertilizers, herbicides, and pesticides to solve various problems. The higher the yields were, the better the bottom line was. But the bottom line kept shrinking. While input costs kept rising, grain prices didn't rise at the same rate. Perpetually lower prices and higher input costs bankrupted many individual farmers. Due to Hutterites' economy of scale and their mixed farming enterprises, they were able to compete with most large corporate farms and continue growing. And they are still growing. Low priced grain is fed to the steers, hogs, chickens, geese, ducks, and turkeys. While an average mixed farm may run only one to three operations, the colonies can run several, because they have the labor readily available. Farming is no longer a simple business. Twenty years ago, wheat, barley, and oats were the Canadian colonies' main crops. Because of higher prices for specialty "cash crops," however, other agricultural commodities were introduced in the late 1970's and the 1980's. Some of these crops are canola, sunflowers, flax, and peas.

With changes in farming and lifestyle came higher costs for everything, including colony expansion. A Hutterite community branching out today needs a tremendous amount of capital. By the time a new colony has purchased the quotas, land, trucks, tractors, and equipment, and built the houses, barns and shops, the capital it saved in the years before branching out is "sunk" (invested) into the new colony, while both colonies have gone several million dollars into debt. Although a Hutterite colony is able to shave a substantial amount off the cost because they don't pay wages to their people, today it may cost eight to fourteen million dollars to establish a new colony. The Hutterite way of life depends upon—in fact, is driven by—its economic structure. Without a sound financial base, a colony could not determine the considerable independence required for its way of life, and Hutterite society would collapse.

When a colony's population reaches around 120 or 130, it is ready to branch out. By then, the elders may have spent several years trying to secure the land needed to establish a new colony because finding a suitable block of land often takes some time. A colony branching out assumes the financial responsibility for the land payments and the construction of all the buildings and facilities on the new colony. The construction usually takes two to three years. At that stage, nobody knows if he or she will move to the new colony or stay at the old one. This is good. Not knowing serves as a positive incentive for people to work hard and do the best job they can. Once the major facilities of the new colony are almost complete, the old colony is ready to split. Before drawing lots, families are placed under each of the two preachers. Great care is taken to insure that both groups have an equal number of people of both sexes and age distribution. No matter how hard people try to be fair, it doesn't always turn out that way. Colony members are not always happy with the outcome of the split. In the late 1970s, one Saskatchewan colony's branching out was delayed several weeks because members couldn't reach a consensus. Elders from other colonies had to step in to mediate.

With the division carefully worked out, the next stage is to divide the colony's assets, including equipment, machinery, and livestock. Consideration is given to what each community's challenges will be. Today, whether a colony has existed for a hundred years or ten, its houses, barns, and shops have been built to conform to the latest standards. Twenty years ago, quite a few colonies were at a different level of modernity. A new colony automatically acquired new buildings while the mother colony was left with older ones. Inevitably, these had to be remodeled if one community was to maintain the same standards enjoyed by all colonies. While each colony is autonomous in its own development and financial obligations, the competition among Hutterites ensures that the colonies evolve more or less at the same rate. Because of bad timing, poorer land, a dryer climate, and sometimes poor management, some colonies struggle financially. Without periodic help from the more stable communities through interest free loans, a few colonies would go bankrupt or would not be able to afford branching out, resulting in what happened at Radichev in the Ukraine. In time, the colony's economy would break down and its members disband. In the 1980s, due to bad timing, two colonies in Saskatchewan (Estuary and Star City) had to auction off a sizable portion of their land holdings and farm equipment in order to pay their debts. This was distressing not only to Hutterite communities, but also to other individual farmers. Hutterites are seen as pillars of financial strength. These colonies' failure showed that in a changing marketplace, financial vibrancy could not be taken for granted.

On the human level, branching out is often a traumatic experience for individuals and families. It is understandable that thirty years ago people hoped and prayed that God would send them to the new colony at the time of branching out, where everything was new. I remember when Springside Colony branched out in 1968. Everyone in my family hoped that we would be on the side that moved to the new colony. An older cousin told my brothers, sisters, and me that at Baildon, people no longer would need to bathe in a washtub. Instead, we would open a tap and the water would sprinkle from the ceiling. For a six-year-old, this was exciting news—reason for wanting to move. But to some people, showers probably didn't mean that much. They knew that eventually Springside Colony would get showers, too. Moving meant being suddenly wrenched away from kin, friends, and the only place a person had known for all his or her life. John Hostetler wrote: "Only the will of God is strong enough to

separate family members—parents from older children, brother from brother—and break personal and sentimental ties. The individual will must be subordinated to the will of the community."

While showers were an exciting concept for me, they too came with a price. It meant splitting with my closest pals. Never again would we live in the same colony. Paul Waldner was my best friend. He was a year older than I was. We spent many hours together. Our favorite summertime activity was sneaking up behind dragonflies and grabbing their "tails." Older boys often trapped magpies and gophers. A pair of magpie legs or a single gopher tail fetched a nice bounty of five cents or a jawbreaker when brought to the *wiet* (colony treasurer). But I don't think Paul and I killed even one dragonfly! We loved dragonflies. Flitting about among the rose hip bushes and tall prairie grasses, they were fascinating, and they seemed such mythical creatures to us. The large ones were called "choppers," because they looked like helicopters. After the split in 1968, circumstances were such that Paul and I never saw each other again. I visited Springside when I was sixteen years old, but by then, Paul had left the colony. I haven't seen him since the split, and most likely wouldn't recognize him if I saw him. In retrospect, the showers at Baildon seem extremely trivial!

Often separation is a good thing, though. In fact, this is one reason why the Hutterites have survived for so many years. Branching out brings about a renewal. A fresh landscape and a new start every fifteen to twenty years invigorate people. At the branching out of a colony, the population is suddenly half of what it was. People have to work "like crazy," but they also get a chance, particularly men, to advance to higher levels of management. And it keeps the peace. Often, after a colony branches out, individuals whose personalities clashed while they lived in the same colony, and were "each other's worst enemy," become "the best of friends."

Every community, due to periodic division, goes through economic and population cycles. After the division, both colonies are several million dollars in debt because of the cost involved to establish the new colony. It takes a colony several years to pay off its debts, after which it immediately begins to save the capital required for the next branching out. By the time the financial resources are built up, it is almost time to split up again. This would be easy enough to manage if generations of colonies stayed at the same financial level. A typical village or town grows slowly over a long period, and then may eventually decline. But not a Hutterite colony. It is in a perpetual forward motion, always moving toward expansion. It is inevitable that a colony will eventually reach its maximum population and will need to establish a new colony. Today, the dining hall alone can cost a half-million dollars to build. Competition ensures that no colony will go backward in standards or stay too far behind the others in modernity.

For a colony to be able to branch out at the opportune time, it must handle its assets very carefully. Its economy works best with a population of sixty to 125 people. Today, the typical economy of a colony is centered on fewer commodities than thirty years ago. Most Hutterite communities no longer strive for total efficiency. The cost of manufactured goods is low compared to the value of the labor that would be required if Hutterites manufactured the goods themselves. For that reason, certain trades are either no longer a requirement, or are no longer full-time occupations. The best example I can give is that of shoemaking. Twenty-five years ago the colony shoemaker manufactured all the shoes the community needed. It was a full-time occupation. Today, however, it is much cheaper to buy commercially made shoes. While he may still make a few shoes during slow winter months, the shoemaker mostly spends time repairing them. At best, shoemaking today is a part-time job, and the shoemaker has another job such as plumber, electrician, gooseman, or tractor operator. Quite often, this part-time job is given to a semi-retired man in his fifties. The market economy has more or less shifted people's skills to areas where they are the most valuable for the colony's economy.

The changes have affected women's work as well. The most obvious example is peeling potatoes. Twenty years ago, the bell at the community dining hall rang once or twice a week to call the women together to peel a few day's supply of potatoes. Today, one woman can do the job with an automatic potato peeling machine. Even further back in time, women used to split

feathers on long winter evenings. The wing feathers of geese (saved at butchering time) were pulled apart and the vane part used for pillows, quilts, and mattresses. The shaft or quill was discarded. This activity afforded the women social interaction on long winter evenings. There were other group activities in the home such as spinning and rug-making. Today, however, a woman will make rugs on her computerized sewing machine, which allows her to sew a multitude of intricate patterns and stitches. Or she may make a rug from a piece of carpet. The result is more time spent at home with her family. Families are smaller today because of a reduced birthrate starting around 1965. Therefore, family relations are stronger. With fewer family members (five to seven children), parents are closer to their children, often to the point of spoiling them, by colony standards.

Often problems arise when a colony has a disproportionate number of young men. Baildon Colony (near Moose Jaw, Saskatchewan), where I grew up, is a prime example. From the mid-1970s to the early 1980s we had more men on the field than were needed. For a few years, far too many of our summer days were spent on the fields, picking rocks. We sat around a lot, playing cards and listening to the radio. Men in their mid-to-late twenties weren't ready to retire from running the larger tractors, combines, and swathers. At that stage of Baildon's population cycle, these men couldn't advance to the stock jobs, because these were held by men in their thirties and early forties, who weren't ready to retire. Incentives or feelings of accomplishment among our young people were dangerously low. Baildon was certainly not the only colony with such problems. Neither was the result always the same. But when young men started leaving Baildon Colony to pursue other interests, it seemed as though they were far less attached to the colony life back home than men from other colonies. In a period of about nine years, Baildon Colony lost fifteen young men to the outside world. People leaving colonies was in itself nothing new. For many years, young men had left their communities and then returned. In most colonies, this is still the situation. In my colony's case, however, of all the men who left since 1979, only two have returned. Even two women left and did not return.

I have pondered over this many times,

and have decided that several factors contributed to the problem. The most obvious one was the disproportionate number of young men that I already mentioned. Another factor was that Baildon was somewhat isolated from the other colonies. We had fewer young visitors from other colonies. Almost all the young people at Baildon were cousins to one another. Falling in love with a cousin is dangerous, because there is no future in it. Marriages between cousins are not allowed among Hutterites. Young men and women need each other. Otherwise, life doesn't make much sense to them. When I was nineteen, the boys at Baildon discovered Vanguard Colony, one of the nearest Lehrerleit colonies to Baildon. However, getting a trip started to Vanguard was like pulling teeth. If we wanted to get there, we had to steal the truck or wait until married people initiated a trip. These were rare, though, because few people at Baildon had close relatives at Vanguard. Wouldn't it have made more sense to allow us to go with a chaperon? Young people didn't care how they got there, as long as they did. There were other problems. Whenever a rumor got underway about the Baildon boys, it would ricochet back from the Lethbridge colonies two weeks later, blown out of proportion to such a degree you had to laugh. One time, after the preacher found and destroyed a television set, the rumor flying around in the Lethbridge colonies was that the preacher had confiscated fifteen television sets! For some crazy reason a few people from our own colony resorted to spreading the rumors.

There were other reasons many of us lost interest in our community's affairs. Aside from making private money by working out occasionally for neighbors, we trapped foxes and coyotes in the fall and winter. While Hutterite boys have always made a bit of money on the side by trapping, our lucrative pastime coincided with extremely high fur prices. A single coyote pelt sent to the Hudson's Bay Fur Auction in Montreal could earn the trapper as much as $380. To send and receive mail, we rented private post office boxes in Moose Jaw. Whereas in the early years in Alberta, some colonies had to trap foxes, coyotes, and badgers, because the animals' sheer numbers were threatening the colonies' chicken and goose stocks,

we trapped solely to make money. Some of us caught twenty to fifty pelts every fall and winter. The generation of young men before us had tried to trap, but the most they ever caught were one or two animals each season. Perhaps it was because they couldn't invest much time in trapping, or maybe it was because they didn't have the incentive of high fur prices like we did. If they received thirty dollars for a coyote pelt, they were lucky. Our group took trapping to a new level. The boys divided the colony's and our nearest neighbors' land, each of us claiming an area on a first-come-first-serve basis. When I started trapping, the close-by land was all claimed, so I had to prospect for new land, some of which was five miles from the colony. The competition among us was fierce. We read books on trapping, ordered special lures through the mail, and spoiled the foxes and coyotes by feeding them juicy chicken and goose guts. Three weeks before trapping season opened, we began carrying or hauling the guts to the fields. They were perfect bait. When the season opened, the foxes and coyotes had no idea what hit them. Once you trapped a family member, you were guaranteed to catch the rest that came to feed at the gut pile.

Carrying a five-gallon pail filled with guts three or more miles across soft summer-fallow was no easy task. Eventually, some of us invested in bicycles, then even motorcycles. Bicycles and motorcycles were forbidden in the colony, so we had to keep them hidden. I ran half a mile to where my bicycle was hidden, which took me to where my motorcycle was, in an abandoned shack three miles from the colony. After I bought my motorcycle, I expanded my trap-line, traveling fifteen to twenty miles every day.

Aside from trapping, I devoted my free time to drawing cartoons and reading books that I bought every time I went to Moose Jaw. Other boys developed more expensive habits. With no experience in handling those amounts of cash, some young people grew restless. Alcohol scared the hell out of me. A few older and already baptized men (who were in a position to be role models) drank too much, and that did nothing to help younger people get a sense of what a good Hutterite was supposed to be. In any case, too much free time to earn private money and to watch TV, and not having enough responsibilities at a crucial time in our development, distracted many of us from colony affairs.

Elders, alarmed that so many young people were leaving the colonies, had to relax a few rules. Fifteen years ago, young people caught with skates and hockey sticks were punished. Today, they walk across the yard with their hockey sticks and skates in broad daylight. Our crew once rented a car to travel to other colonies to play hockey. At one Hutterite community in southern Alberta, the preacher ordered that the ice on the dugout be destroyed. I don't think that would happen today. The elders look the other way, hoping that by giving in a little, the young people will stay in the colony.

So far, Hutterites have been remarkably successful in keeping very old traditions alive, and at the same time they move forward in the modern world. Keeping the balance is no easy task. Changes in technology alter traditional work patterns, and a community must adapt accordingly. Within a colony's population cycle, people's dedication to the community has its ebbs and flows. This is why a Hutterite colony cannot afford to become stagnant in the area of productivity.

Neither can it stray very far from traditional values and beliefs.

Elders have often asked themselves: what went wrong? Why aren't young people returning to the colony as easily as the previous generation of weggelufene (runaways) did? Was it the elders' fault? What could they have done differently?

I think the situation was due to human cycles operating in a fast changing world, where attachment to traditions had increasingly less importance in young people's minds. We were caught in a generation gap. As a result, the community suffered severe losses.

As one zooms into the microcosm of a community, then zooms out to the macrocosm of the larger society, the whole picture of the Hutterites' challenges unfolds. Sociologists thrive on studying socioeconomic relationships such as these. Since 1950, many studies have been done of Hutterite life against the backdrop of twentieth century North American society. What happened at Baildon does not necessarily mean that Hutterites' future is in danger. Cycles usually correct themselves. Having survived this long, I think Hutterites will continue to be successful far into the next century.

When East Met West

One part of Hutterite history in the 20th century deals with the marriage between two different communal societies that ultimately ended in divorce because the two groups were not compatible. This union also caused a schism in the Hutterite church in the early 1990s. Many people were hurt and profoundly shaken in its wake, and the aftermath of the breakup will continue into the next century. The outside world first became aware of trouble brewing in the Hutterite colonies when in 1989, laying aside Peter Riedemann's instruction in his *Confession of Faith* (1540), Schmiedeleit Hutterites in Manitoba were caught up in a lawsuit. Church brother against church brother this time. What made the suit even more alarming: the bishop of the Schmiedeleit had thrown the first punch! By then, much wrangling between colony members, the fudging of truths, and abuses by people in positions of power had already transpired. True Hutterite Christian community, where the common good of the whole is the golden principle, had taken a back seat to politics and authoritarian leadership. The whole set of issues was a convoluted mess that pitted preacher against preacher, brother against brother, sister against sister—literally tearing families apart. It took several years until enough of the story was known in order that an outsider could put it into perspective.

The Bruderhof, or Society of Brothers, was the catalyst that ultimately brought about the schism among the Schmiedeleit Hutterites. The Society was founded in Germany, in 1920, by a charismatic theologian named Eberhard Arnold. Seeking to create a Utopian community in the chaotic aftermath of World War I, he and his wife, Emmy Arnold, attracted a circle of like-minded individuals, many of whom were drawn from the German Youth Movement, a loose affiliation of internationalists, pacifists, socialists, and Christians. Not even knowing that Hutterites existed in North America, the group began studying old Hutterite writings. When Eberhard Arnold learned of the Hutterites in North America, he made a pilgrimage to South Dakota and the Canadian prairie provinces in 1930. He spent a year studying among the Hutterites. Subsequently, he was ordained as a Hutterite minister at Standoff Colony in Alberta and commissioned "to proclaim the Word of God" and "gather the zealous" in Germany.

After returning to Germany, Arnold began modeling his small group's structure along Hutterite communal living patterns, imitating Hutterite practices more or less in worship, dress, child rearing, and so on. Arnold died in 1935. His group, because of Nazi persecution, later fled, first to Liechtenstein, then to England. They were there only five years due to anti-German sentiment. Canada and America rejected their overtures for asylum; as a result between 1940 and 1941, most of their members immigrated to Paraguay. Financial support was given by some Hutterite colonies in the hope that the Society of Brothers would be faithful members of the traditional Hutterite movement. But funding was cut after a delegation of two Hutterite ministers visited the Paraguayan colonies in 1949. They found that the Society of Brothers allowed activities such as tobacco smoking, music, folk dancing, watching movies, and letting women attend council meetings, among others. These activities were forbidden in the Hutterite colonies. While this did not make the Society of Brothers any less dedicated to community, it showed some fundamental differences between them and the Hutterites. The relationship between the Society of Brothers and the Hutterites was strained.

By 1953, there were three Bruderhof settlements in Paraguay, with a combined total of about 700 members. After World War II, the United States was more hospitable than it had been during the war, and in 1954, the first Bruderhof community, known as Woodcrest, was opened at Rifton, New York. Later, a series of internal conflicts erupted over intellectual and spiritual issues and more than half of the members departed from the Paraguayan settlements, some voluntarily, some because they were expelled by the leaders. About 200 people later returned to the Bruderhof communities in the United States. The Paraguayan settlements were closed. Smaller groups in England and Germany also disbanded. By 1962, the Society of Brothers resided solely in the United States.

But even before the last communities in Paraguay had been closed, the Society of Brothers in America had experienced a union of sorts with the Hutterites—which had gone bad. In 1955, the group appealed to the traditional Hutterites for reconciliation. Forest River Colony, near Inkster, North Dakota, which already had its share of dissident members, was sympathetic to the Society of Brothers. They went against the general Hutterite consensus and opened their community, inviting Bruderhof members into Forest River. Thirty-six Bruderhofers arrived from the east, including nurses, teachers, lawyers, and four ministers.

The union was disastrous to the Hutterites. Ruth Baer Lambach, an ex-Hutterite who now lives in Chicago, was a teenager at Forest River at the time. She recalls that the Bruderhof "was a patchwork community of eccentrics, intellectuals, dissident seekers of truth, and creative practitioners of radical Christianity," who took over Forest River "like a hurricane." They virtually took over the Schmiedeleit. The resident Hutterite preacher, Andreas Hofer, returned to the parent colony in Manitoba with forty of his people. Schmiedeleit ministers then stepped in and excommunicated the Society of Brothers from Forest River "for causing disunity and divisiveness and for wrong-doing." Thirty-six Hutterites dissidents also ended up leaving Forest River, some going east to live at Woodcrest. Forest River, placed on probation, was left with great financial difficulties, and only a handful of people remained.

Although they recovered somewhat, the remaining Hutterites soon realized that if they were to survive as a Hutterite people, they would need to reconcile with the Hutterite Church. After sending many letters of apology and pleas for help to the Hutterites in Manitoba, they did receive help. Sam Kleinsasser, the head preacher of Sturgeon Creek Colony made a trip to Alberta to obtain financial help from the Alberta colonies in order to help Forest River get back on its feet. It was given. A preacher named Paul Maendel was sent to Forest River to organize the repairing of buildings and to reorganize Forest River Colony after years of financial crisis. Other Hutterites were sent to Forest River to repopulate it, and the colony was once more in good standing with the Hutterite church.

For twenty years relations between the Hutterites and the Bruderhofs were strained. Those Hutterites related to the apostates who had joined the Society of Brothers never gave up hope that their relatives would someday return to the Hutterite church, staying in contact with them through letter writing and occasional visits. In 1964, Heini Arnold, son of the Bruderhof's founder and now leader of the group, visited the Hutterite preachers and personally apologized for the division. In 1973, the Society of Brothers once again initiated contact, hoping to obtain a formal reconciliation with the Hutterites. By now, some of the dissidents who had left Forest River and joined the Society of Brothers were pushing for a reunion with the Hutterites. They either had guilty consciences for abandoning the Hutterite church or truly felt that a blending of the groups' cultures could benefit both groups. A year later, Heini Arnold and representatives of the Bruderhofs met with seventy-one Hutterite ministers from all three Leit at a colony in Manitoba, where the Society of Brothers made their appeal. The Hutterites decided—or were persuaded—to re-admit the dissidents and Bruderhofers on a trial basis. This was a soul-searching decision on the part of the Hutterites. Optimism prevailed, however, because elders hoped the union would prosper. The Dariusleit and Lehrerleit, who had been cautious about this development from the start, continued to be wary. But eventually they too warmed to the idea.

With one foot in the door, the Society of Brothers sought people within the Hutterite communities to champion their cause. They found the man they were looking for, Jakob Kleinsasser, a charismatic and persuasive Schmiedeleit minister living at Crystal Spring Colony in Manitoba. He turned out to be the greatest mover and shaker among the western Hutterites, especially after he became the bishop of the Schmiedeleit in 1978.

Many Bruderhof members had no desire to join the Hutterites, wear the traditional Hutterite clothes and adapt to their ideology. But Bruderhof leaders managed to compel most of the communities' members to conform to their views. A Hutterite scholar recently theorized that the reason the Society of Brothers wanted in to the Hutterite church was because "they didn't have a religion." Although the Bruderhofs were successful in their venture of manufacturing high quality children's toys (Community Playthings), they "had to latch onto a larger body of religious literature, theology, philosophy, and so on." The traditional Hutterites (the west) had that, the Society of Brothers (the east) did not.

At first it seemed as though the Schmiedeleit had done the right thing. Some of their ministers "fell head over heels in love" with the Society of Brothers' system of communal living, particularly "with the childlike submission and unreserved obedience by the common people to a hierarchy-type government." Other aspects of the Bruderhofs showed a strength that the Hutterites admired, although with reserve. The Bruderhof leaders were prepared to test the beliefs of their members and children against the world. If people left the community, they left. The Bruderhofs were not afraid to send people with doubts about their faith out into the world to test their convictions. The Hutterites saw this as a sign of remarkable vitality and confidence in the Society of Brothers' faith.

Younger Hutterites were particularly enthusiastic. In the Bruderhof communities, women were allowed to participate in community discussions, children were allowed to attend local schools outside the Bruderhofs after Grade 9, and men were given more leeway in how they used their education and skills beyond agriculture. Furthermore, the Bruderhofers' warm and fervent faith encouraged joyful prayer, community singing, and stirring music. People displayed more openness and shared their feelings. In comparison, the old-fashioned spirituality of the Hutterites felt cold, formal, and homogenous.

The Bruderhof communities were also involved with outreach and missionary work. In 1988, the Bruderhofers organized a conference on social responsibilities, and gave workshops on hunger and homelessness, abortion and drugs, war and racism. And their children delivered food to slum districts in New York. Outreach activities of this proportion had been abandoned by the Hutterites more than 200 years earlier.

What Hutterites underestimated, though, was the Bruderhofs' different history and character. The traditional Hutterites had been born to well-established orthodox traditions and customs and knew no other. The Bruderhofs, however, while experiencing a regular flow of recruits, were still working out their doctrine and newly educating their people. Recruits, coming from different backgrounds and levels of education, had more baggage left over from their former lives. This meant that community leaders had to be more forceful and authoritarian in installing their codes of behavior. With manufacturing as the Bruderhofs' main source of income, the communities were bound up to a centralized, top-down management style of control. Woodcrest served as the headquarters for the other communities. (In 1998, there were a total of six Bruderhof communities in the States of New York, Pennsylvania, and Connecticut. There is also one such community in England. The group has about 2500 members.)

Having lived a good number of years in a golden era, with virtually no persecution to speak of other than the odd restrictions on land acquisitions in Manitoba, many Schmiedeleit had become lax and complacent. Other Schmiedeleit, those who had more desire for spiritual growth, were abandoning the old Hutterite faith for a new "Born Again" experience, which didn't necessarily include submission to a denominational church, nor living in the colony. Elders thought, perhaps the energy and infusion of new ideas from the Society of Brothers would be the answer to their prayers. Some Schmiedeleit Hutterites, however, were able to discern very early that this union would result in chaos. "No good will come of this!" they said.

Meanwhile, Jacob Kleinsasser had risen to full power in his church. When he became the bishop of the Schmiedeleit, he gained command of the ship he had wanted for so many years. Hutterites believe their bishops to be appointed to the helm of the church by God. A bishop is not considered infallible, however, by virtue of his having been chosen by God, he is thought to be accountable directly to God Himself and therefore his order must be obeyed. A bishop making a wrong judgement call from time to time is inevitable. However, most bishops will not abuse their power. In this fast changing world, where every boundary seems to be constantly pushed to the limit, a Hutterite bishop has tremendous challenges. He must have skill, tact, and resolution.

Jacob Kleinsasser may have had good intentions. Some Hutterites later felt that perhaps the mess between the Society of Brothers and the Schmiedeleit, with Jacob Kleinsasser as the kingpin, was orchestrated by a higher power, that God wanted to wake up a moribund people and bring about a reformation. An analysis given by sociologists gives a more satisfactory answer. The Bruderhofs' livelihood was solely manufacturing, and the Hutterites' economy was still derived mostly from farming. The bishop saw the difficulties in acquiring sufficient land, dairy and egg quotas, and so on. Thinking ahead, he was looking to the eastern communities as models for the non-agricultural communal life that the Hutterites might someday need to adopt.

Jacob Kleinsasser also initiated a push for higher education, which he intensely felt that Hutterites needed. In the eastern communities, children complete high school, and often go to university. Kleinsasser wanted the same for the traditional Hutterites. He wanted to see Hutterite school teachers, all with degrees, teaching the provincial curriculum to colony children. Since then, much of this has happened. Hutterite communities in Manitoba have entered a new phase of education. Unlike before, now parents and elders are encouraging young people to stay in school and to complete high school. In 1994, twenty-one Hutterites entered Brandon University's newly developed Hutterite Education Program. These people obtained their teaching certificates in 1998. I think they are doing the prudent thing, fortifying their traditional apprentice teaching methods with higher education.

By his own accounts, Jacob Kleinsasser intended to teach the Bruderhof communities the true Hutterite way. "The Woodcrest people are not introducing new ideas. They are learning from us, how to be become good Hutterites!" This is how he countered when his critics pointed out he was pushing his programs of good relations with the Bruderhofs too far. To the people in the east, who now were promoting themselves as the Hutterian Society of Brothers, the bishop had became a hero, a modern-day Jacob Hutter. Marriages between the Schmiedeleit and the Bruderhofers had also begun taking place. Kleinsasser's daughter Dora was one of about twenty Manitoba women to marry into the Bruderhofs. Christoph Arnold, the successor to the Bruderhof throne after his father Heini died in 1982, put Jacob Kleinsasser almost at par with Jesus Christ.

From an outsider's perspective, the exchange of ideas and the reformation that appeared to be going on seemed like a good thing. But what kind of new spirit was it that would support lawsuits, initiated by the bishop, of all people? Dragging a church member into the world court had absolutely nothing to do with the Hutterite way! Who was teaching whom? Were the blind leading the blind? Where had the bishop learned such drastic, un-Hutterite tactics?

The conflict at first seemed to stem from the so-called Daniel Hofer Case, for this was the catalyst that brought the problems brewing in the Schmiedeleit colonies to the attention of the outside world. Daniel Hofer, a Hutterite from Lakeside Colony in Manitoba, had invented a wet-dry hog feeder system a few years earlier. Jacob Kleinsasser's colony (Crystal Spring), going against another Hutterite golden rule that says, "what's mine is yours, and what's yours is mine," by most accounts stole the design from Lakeside Colony and beat Daniel Hofer to the patent office. Patenting a product is, of course, a prudent thing to do in a democratic society. It is a standard procedure inventors or investors follow in order to prevent any Tom, Dick, and Harry from making the product themselves. The Hutterites, however, are accustomed to freely sharing their knowledge among their colonies. Among them, no patent was ever needed. Copying another colony's innovative idea was nothing new. Daniel Hofer claimed that his intent from the start had been to share the hog feeder design with the entire Hutterite order, with royalties going to Lakeside.

Crystal Spring Colony found itself owners of a patent that was worthless, because colonies left and right had copied the design and manufactured their own feeders. To be fair, Crystal Spring likely had already invested a lot of money to set up manufacturing of the product. This problem showed a weak link in Hutterite property distribution. On the one hand, property is co-owned by all members in a colony. On the other hand, each colony is fiercely autonomous in its dealings. A patent is property. The colonies that were copying the patented feeder design were doing so illegally. At that point it might have been useful to enter into discussion about trade rules and how they applied to intercolony affairs. Instead, the management at Crystal Spring chose to handle the problem in an underhanded way. In what can only be interpreted as a wicked move, considering Hutterite doctrine, they sold the patent for a dollar to a firm outside the colony, who in turn refused the right of Daniel Hofer's colony, as well as many others, to continue making and selling the feeders. Lawsuits followed. Some colonies, wanting to avoid problems, settled out of court, paying around $10,000 each. All legal bills were shared by the outside firm (the patent owners) and Crystal Spring, but they also divided up the money received from the settlements. Crystal Spring Colony had found a way to profit from their venture after all.

Daniel Hofer accused the bishop and other church elders of corruption and underhanded financial dealings in order to bail out their various business ventures that had gone sour, including a failed pig abattoir at Neepawa, which lost eight million dollars in 1986-87. The bishop turned around and excommunicated Daniel Hofer. But this man didn't capitulate like everybody else did. He refused to leave Lakeside. That is when Kleinsasser took drastic measures. He sued in civil court to evict the Hofer family and their supporters from the colony. Daniel Hofer, not to be outdone, countersued. Although he lost, he opened a whole new set of complex issues by bringing to the court accusations against the bishop and his associates. Kleinsasser had unwittingly stepped into a trap that would force him to reveal more of his questionable dealings than ever imagined. Daniel Hofer later appealed his case, and in 1992, the Supreme Court sided

with him. In the interim, numerous financial forays came to light that took disastrous turns under Kleinsasser's general stewardship, through which colonies had lost untold millions of dollars. The allegations were that Kleinsasser and others had created numerous businesses and started money management practices which, while they looked good on the surface, were designed to fleece other colonies. Kleinsasser insisted that it was his intent always to "take from the richer colonies to help the poorer colonies."

It is simply beyond the scope of this book to expound on these ventures. The crux of it all, though, was that the Schmiedeleit, under Kleinsasser's leadership, and influenced by the eastern communities, gravitated towards the idea of central control. Church taxes were introduced to build up a church fund, and other similar money-making schemes were gradually introduced. These measures often lead to a forced submission on the part of various communities in order to achieve this new style of financial control. The autonomy and democracy individual Hutterite colonies had enjoyed for so long had become severely impaired.

The bishop's office carries sweeping powers. Generally, these powers of office are used only sparingly, but Kleinsasser took a more heavy-handed approach, intervening in internal affairs of colonies like nobody before him. In one conflict situation at Rainbow Colony near Winnipeg, Kleinsasser refused to let the colony elect its own minister in the typical fashion. Instead, he sent an overseer of his own. The people at Rainbow Colony rejected the overseer, so Kleinsasser seized the colony's quarter-million dollar bank account, then instructed the people to vacate the premises. Like Daniel Hofer, they too refused to budge. Through this kind of behavior the bishop set in motion a rift that literally tore through the Hutterite communities like a prairie fire, ripping apart communities and families, as people were forced to take sides or risk excommunication. Depending on whose side a preacher was on, he may or may not have been allowed to preach in his own community. The Hutterite colonies are close-knit communities and people are related to one another, which compounded the impact these developments had. People who didn't side with the bishop were removed from their positions.

Those who protested were expelled. People were expelled for the smallest transgressions. Even some marriages were torn apart—wives left their husbands and moved back to their home community.

The Dariusleit and Lehrerleit, however, were not duped. They weren't as close to the situation, and had the benefit of seeing it from a distance. Many Schmiedeleit have always looked down on the Dariusleit and Lehrerleit, particularly on the Lehrerleit, thinking themselves superior and more enlightened. However, time would prove who was more successful. The two groups were shocked at Jacob Kleinsasser's brazen actions when he initiated the string of lawsuits. They were ready to take him to task at their biannual meeting in 1990. However, Jacob Kleinsasser didn't show up, despite being the president of the three-Leit conference. He sent a proxy instead. Consequently, the Dariusleit and Lehrerleit removed Kleinsasser from his largely honorary position. In a letter addressed to "Whom It May Concern," the Lehrerleit later wrote about his overall conduct in the course of these events: "His (Kleinsasser's) demeanor was one of arrogance; aloofness and overbearing superiority to say the least; belittling the Lehrerleit and Dariusleit, touting the virtues of the Arnoldleit (another name for the Society of Brothers)."

There were other practices that had crept into the Schmiedeleit colonies which the Lehrerleit and Dariusleit criticized. They were alarmed at hearing that some Schmiedeleit were now taking babies into church (children under six years of age do not go to church in traditional Hutterite colonies). They were dismayed about live music at religious services and weddings, and about the use of torches and candles in worship. In 1990, realizing where this was all coming from, the Dariusleit and Lehrerleit presented a list of ten particulars concerning un-Hutterite practices to the Society of Brothers, along with a list of other grievances. With that they also formally revoked the 1974 reunification of the Bruderhofs: "out of fear that such forbidden sins may slowly infiltrate into our colonies." The traditionalists went on to ask the Society of Brothers "to stop using and tarnishing the Hutterite image with your anti-Hutterian deeds."

By 1992, Jacob Kleinsasser's actions had also won him a lot of opposition among the Schmiedeleit, who were having second thoughts about the Bruderhofs in the east. For awhile it had seemed as if Kleinsasser had been successful in replacing the old time-honored ways of leadership with the new style. He was, after all, the bishop appointed by God. His desire to introduce eastern practices, however, meant dismantling and discarding Hutterite traditions and cultural habits. Eventually, more and more Schmiedeleit (the more traditionally-minded) sided with the late Joseph Wipf from South Dakota, who had turned out to be Kleinsasser's biggest rival. Officially, Joseph Wipf had been elected as the bishop's assistant. Wipf called upon the Lehrerleit and Dariusleit for help. After several meetings, assurance of support was given in a letter signed by seventy-eight Lehrerleit and Dariusleit ministers, including the bishops of the two Leit.

In December, 1992, some 170 Schmiedeleit ministers met and presented twelve long-standing grievances against Kleinsasser's leadership. Kleinsasser asked for a vote of confidence. His own supporters, probably realizing what the result of the referendum would be, tried to talk him out of it. Kleinsasser persisted, however, and the preachers voted. More than half of them voted to remove Kleinsasser from his position, and agreed that he was no longer an elder of the Hutterian Brethren Church (95 preachers were against Kleinsasser, 75 were for him, and the number of preachers against him increased after they had a chance to talk with their people and council brethren back home at their respective colonies). Once again Kleinsasser's tactics had backfired. But he rejected the outcome of the vote. So now there were two factions of Schmiedeleit, each claiming to hold the true title to the Hutterite church.

The Kleinsasser group met at Crystal Spring Colony in March, 1993, where they were told that they could no longer preach at colonies that did not recognize Kleinsasser's leadership. For the preachers who did not recognize Kleinsasser's leadership, Kleinsasser also refused to renew credentials that allowed them to perform marriages. Licenses to solemnize marriages expire every two years, and Kleinsasser, as senior elder of the Schmiedeleit, was the only one authorized to renew them. This created great inconveniences for people. But, ultimately, the problems were resolved when the majority of the Hutterite colonies (who opposed Kleinsasser) signed their name on a document that amended the Hutterite constitution of 1950 and reaffirmed their allegiance to the Hutterian Brethren Church. Subsequently, on September 13, 1993, Vital Statistics of Manitoba designated two Hutterite preachers as Governing Authorities of the Hutterian Brethren Church, who were then able to authorize clergy to solemnize marriages in Manitoba. At this time, or shortly after, Joseph Wipf's Schmiedeleit group also broke all ties with the Society of Brothers in the east. In a letter written by Samuel Kleinsasser (the former bishop's brother) of Concord Colony, near Winnipeg, the group outlined their grievances against the Society. Through their spokesman, leaders of the colonies pointed out that, while it was not their "intention to judge and condemn," they felt compelled to also part company because East and West were not compatible with each other.

Jacob Kleinsasser's group was offensively nicknamed "Oilers" by people on the opposite side, after an oil well fiasco, one of Kleinsasser's business deals that had gone bad. Joseph Wipf's group, in turn, was nicknamed "Gibbs," after Donald Gibb, a banker who had documented Jacob Kleinsasser's business acumen over the years. The banker's thick volume of documents and bank statements helped the Hutterites wade through the many bungles and crooked deals that had occurred.

Although the Society of Brothers had tried to come to Jacob Kleinsasser's defense, their position was weakened by their no longer being allowed to use the Hutterite name. Worse yet, since 1989, their reputation had taken a beating after a former Bruderhof member named Ramón Sender, now living in San Francisco, began circulating a Round Robin letter to people who had been expelled from the Bruderhofs over the years. The letter turned into a newsletter called KIT (Keep It Together). The stories of ex-Bruderhof members showed a vastly different picture than what the Bruderhofs were displaying to the world through their propaganda arm of Plough Publishing House. To be fair, the contributors also had many fond memories, and

the general tone of the stories did become less harsh as time went on: people were healed through the process of sharing their experiences.

In contrast to two of the Bruderhofs' own books, *Torches Together* and *Torches Rekindled*, a former Bruderhof member, Elizabeth Bohlken-Zumpe, released her version of the Bruderhof experience in a book titled *Torches Extinguished*. The Bruderhofs' first book detailed Emmy Arnold's account of the Bruderhof's beginnings in Germany. (Emmy was Zumpe's grandmother.) The second book, later published by the Bruderhofs, sought to show how, through the false leadership of Elizabeth Zumpe's father, Hans Zumpe, the Bruderhof communities lost their "light," and went through "dark years," particularly in Paraguay. Through the efforts of their prophet, Heini Arnold, who managed to overthrow Hans Zumpe, the torches were rekindled in the Bruderhof communities. But that wasn't as important as what was revealed through Elizabeth Zumpe's book. She quoted her grandfather, Eberhard Arnold, the founder of the Bruderhof: "The first generation has the spirit. The second generation, the good example. The third generation, the vivid memory. And the fourth generation is often stuck with all the rules and regulations. This will turn them into a sect—a cult."

By most accounts given by former Bruderhof members, this is what happened. Many of them were expelled from the Bruderhofs, or they left on their own because they couldn't stand the control of the communities. Some of the things that became known showed how the Society of Brothers, under the leadership of Heini Arnold, changed into an authoritarian society. I am sure Heini learned quite a lot from early Hutterite leaders in Moravia, particularly Jacob Hutter, who really had to be strong and firm if his communities were to survive. Jacob Hutter was a humble man, though. At one point in the early days in Moravia, some people in the communities opposed him because they thought he held too strictly to reform. Hutter asked for a vote from the leaders. They voted him out, so he stepped back. Hutter exercised true democracy, not a dictatorship.

Through the stories published in the KIT newsletter and Elizabeth Zumpe's book, the true colors of the Bruderhofs became known. Now it was obvious where Jacob Kleinsasser had acquired his "new" spirit. Zumpe wrote about how hundreds of people were sent away from the Bruderhof communities in a kind of purging, and how, after Eberhard Arnold passed away, they lost their original spirit of love and nurture. Instead, the leaders' main tasks became that of "judging the spirit of the brothers and sisters." They became chasers of evil, searching for interesting sins, usually related to sex, beginning with young children.

Ramón Sender had been prevented from visiting his daughter throughout her childhood. She had remained in the community when he departed. The Bruderhof wouldn't release information about her engagement, marriage, nor the birth of her two children. When she died very suddenly from terminal cancer, he was only notified a month after her death. Bereft, he began gathering information in order to write a book about her life, speaking with several other people who had been expelled from the Bruderhofs. In doing so, he opened a dialogue with people who wanted to share their grievances and hardships. His newsletter grew and soon was being mailed to over three-hundred ex-Bruderhofers.

John Hostetler, emeritus professor living in Pennsylvania, who has researched the Hutterites, the Society of Brothers, and other social and cultural organizations since 1959, is one of the leading scholars of Hutterite life. In an unpublished paper, *The Society of Brothers who call themselves Hutterites: Some Personal Concerns,* he voiced his distress about the Society of Brothers. He wrote: "As a social anthropologist, I have no interest in proving that one system of political economy and innovative community is superior to another." In regards to the Christian community he wrote: "Christianity, it seems to me, can penetrate all economic and cultural systems." Hostetler grew up in an Amish community, and is well aware, as I am, that living in a semi-closed culture often presents emotional and personal difficulties for individuals. Hostetler added: "I have seen the loving support provided by a 'brotherly and sisterly' way of life, as well as the tragedies of division, exclusion, and fragmentation."

In my own life, I have seen and experienced how religion can unite people as well as tear them apart. My resolve—and I have been criticized for that—is to celebrate and champion all the different religions. I believe in allowing all religions from the smallest to the greatest to co-exist rather than upholding a system that teaches one religion for all people.

The Bruderhof communities, as described by many former members, were a "totalitarian, cultic, and coercive" society. Some of the main points of concern John Hostetler voiced in his article were about "the intense interrogation of children, self-annihilation, totalitarian attitudes, rule by descent, and ambiguous beliefs." I do not have space here to expound on all of these in detail, but one that clearly violates Hutterite principles is the intense interrogation of children. Yes, Hutterite children are taught the rules of the community. That is normal. But in the Bruderhof communities (according to Hostetler's findings), in order to create that "pure" community, drastic disciplinary measures were sometimes practiced against children. Young children from the ages of nine to fourteen were interrogated for their sexual fantasies and punished by being placed in isolation for weeks. In like fashion, it was reported, in 1994 at a Schmiedeleit colony in South Dakota that "everyone was forced to dig back into their past to uncover all their sins, even from before baptism. Their confessions were printed up in a booklet and made public, at least within the Hutterite church." This outraged many Hutterites, who found the breach of confidentiality unacceptable behavior.

Like Hostetler, I am not trying to prove that the Hutterite system is any better than any other community's. Neither do I wish to portray the Bruderhofs as evil places. I doubt very much that they are. Unfortunately, it is often the "evil" in someone or something that first catches most adult minds in our society. I would be the first to applaud some of the ways in which the Bruderhofers influenced the Hutterites for the better, particularly in the area of education. Strip away the external parts of any group, and you will find that most human beings all over the world are the same. People in Bruderhof communities, in Hutterite communities, and in cities and towns across the land have the same concerns, the same problems, and the same loves. The human condition is the same everywhere. The problem lies with misguided leaders, who allow their hunger for power to destroy their otherwise good intentions.

By 1995, the Bruderhof leaders had lost confidence in Jacob Kleinsasser, and the relationship between Kleinsasser and Christoph Arnold disintegrated. By now it sounded like a soap opera. In May, 1995, *The Mennonite Reporter* published news about the controversy: "A flurry of angry letters have emerged out of the Hutterite colonies and the Bruderhofs, pointing to an unexpected new controversy and possible split." In the Winter 1995 issue of *The Plough,* Christoph Arnold had fired a volume of accusations against the Hutterites, making sweeping generalizations about alcoholism, premarital sex, legitimacy, and unfaithfulness in marriage. The Bruderhofs themselves were at the time involved in a lawsuit with Palmgrove, a Bruderhof community in Nigeria, which they had helped get started with the financial support of the Canadian Hutterite colonies. Reading the letters, which a researcher in Manitoba faithfully sent to me, I got the impression that all civility had ceased to exist. Ramón Sender's KIT newsletter also published tidbits of information now and then. As a writer, always seeking to discern the truth as best I can, I sometimes questioned the validity of the sources. But I grew to appreciate the candidness and democratic style of the newsletter. When it was announced in January, 1996, that the relationship between Jakob Kleinsassers's Schmiedeleit and the Society of Brothers was dissolved, I realized the KIT newsletter had provided an accurate picture.

As I wrote at the beginning of this chapter, the marriage between the Hutterites and Bruderhofers ended in divorce because of cultural differences that simply could not be overcome. The KIT newsletter reported that the Bruderhof leader had, since 1991, carried a concealed weapon on his person. Other items came to light. The Bruderhofs bought a corporate jet, and were flying the likes of Eddie Van Halen (glamour rockstar) and Sharon Stone (from *Basic Instinct* movie fame), to their many destinations. In 1997, the Bruderhofs launched a lawsuit against Ramón Sender and the KIT crew. It was later dropped when the Bruderhof leaders realized how far

Sender's group would take their case. They even thanked Sender for all the free publicity, and "for making them (the Bruderhofs) famous." These ongoing developments continued to show how different the Hutterites are from the Society of Brothers and how precarious the relationship was from the beginning.

Since the early to mid-1990's the branching of communities had accelerated because of various factions within communities. By splitting earlier, these Hutterites were able to resolve their conflicts. In 1997 an outside building contractor informed that the only way some Hutterites could work together was by having someone like him give them orders, because he was not politically connected.

At the beginning of 1999, the two factions of Schmiedeleit hadn't yet patched up their differences, but marriages between the groups were still allowed. As for the number of communities that officially opposed Jacob Kleinsasser's leadership, the smoke hadn't completely cleared. Most colonies that have branched out in the last few years have officially elected to declare their allegiance with the larger body of Hutterites. At least two thirds of the Schmiedeleit colonies sided with Jake Waldner (Blumengart Colony, Manitoba) the appointed bishop of the Schmiedeleit. The assistant elder to Mr. Waldner, for the American Schmiedeleit, was Jake Wipf (Spring Creek Colony, North Dakota). The legal name for the larger group of Schmiedeleit was established as *Schmiedeleut Conference of the Hutterian Brethren.* Jakob Kleinsasser's associates (representing 55 colonies) did attempt to secure the same name for their group; in early 1999 there was a legal case pending on this issue. It appeared that once again the world courts would end up settling the matter.

After the 1998 printing of *The Hutterites: Lives & Images of a Communal People,* I was made aware of criticism about my coverage of these events by Jacob Kleinsasser's supporters, yet nobody was able to come forward and offer anything new. Kleinsasser's closest supporters appear to deny that he ever did anything wrong, when indeed the evidence has been chronicled and laid bare many times. Thus, I stand by my research and accept that my work is based on the truth.

It is now easier to understand why the Hutterites broke into different groups in Russia and upon settling in North America. The Hutterite lifestyle can survive only in opposition to another group, or the world at large. For their faith to survive and continue to be justified, they need an "evil world" to separate from. Otherwise, there would be no point in being a people apart, as they are. The brief union with the Society of Brothers showed that.

At the end of the century it remains to be seen how much further the Society of Brothers' influence will have on the Hutterites. Jakob Kleinsasser's group appears to have strong leanings towards radical evangelical ideals; members often claim that they represent true Christianity, whereas people from the other group do not. I doubt very much the two groups will ever come together again. Throughout a good part of Mennonite history, when members couldn't come to terms with each other, some people broke away from the mother church and established a daughter Mennonite church. That is why there exist so many different Mennonite churches today. Hutterites are a much smaller group, though. Their population has not yet reached 50,000. How many schisms can they endure? There will always be factions among people, including Hutterites, as people adopt different ideas. The question is: Will all Hutterites who now live communally continue to do so? If so, how much will these communities resemble the original Hutterite communities? Or will they go the way of the Prairieleit?

Prairieleit Hutterites in America—late 19th century. (Photograph—MLA)

Prairieleit Hutterites

In 1880, six years after the first Hutterites arrived in America, 443 of them were living communally in South Dakota. Another 882 had settled on individual homesteads. The latter were called *Prairieleit* (prairie people) by the communal Hutterites. In the Ukraine, after the Schmiedeleit and Dariusleit had renewed communal living, the first group lived at one end of a Hutterite village (Hutterdorf), and the second group lived at the other end. In the middle resided those who had not accepted the community of goods. I think this is symbolic of the relationship between the four Hutterite Leit during their early years in America. They lived near each other, and intermarried. It was common for young Prairieleit women to marry young men in the colony, even though marriages were not encouraged between them. People continued to interact because they were related, shared the same history, and, in the early days, the same faith. There was also business between colonies and the Prairieleit, particularly due to extensive use of Hutterite flourmills by Prairieleit in the late 19th and early 20th centuries. More than a few individuals joined or left colonies. Cultural differences at that stage were minor. Individuals were often accompanied by large families, therefore as many as 200 people may have moved between the prairie and the colonies. Many people chose to settle on individual homesteads because they could acquire a quarter section of free land (160 acres) through the Homestead Act. They were required to live on the property to qualify for ownership, and after five years received free title to the land.

Settlers generally endured considerable stress and familial tension because of geographic relocation and the hard pioneer days in America. But sometimes Hutterite families were split when members disagreed over which direction to go in this new country. Should they settle into communal life? Or should they go the way of private ownership on the prairie? The community offered more security; and problems with the natural elements (prairie fires, grasshoppers, hail, marginal rainfall, winter blizzards, and spring floods) didn't make it any easier for people trying to survive on individual homesteads. The colonies, on the other hand, had many internal problems to work out.

A few people—some due to a troubled conscience, others looking for supernatural signs telling them where to go—had dreams that prompted them to leave or return to the colony. In the late 1880s, one man named Fred Waldner had a dream after dinner one day. In the dream, Fred saw Jesus lying dead in a corner of his house. He was extremely upset. Then he saw Jesus slowly coming to life, not in his own house but in what he recognized as the home of Michael Waldner (the senior elder of the Schmiedeleit) at Bon Homme Colony, near Tabor, South Dakota. Many of Fred's friends and relatives had already joined Bon Homme. Three days later it occurred to him what the dream meant. In a spiritual sense, Jesus was dead in his private house, and would give life to that home only if it was in the colony. Jesus would empower him and give him the supernatural direction if he sold his farm and joined the colony. And this is what he did.

Another man, Joseph Hofer, known as "Yos," was one of the founders of the Wolf Creek Dariusleit community. It is not clear whether or not he had lived communally in the Ukraine. He likely didn't, because his family was one of the more wealthy individual Hutterite families in the Ukraine, and they had not yet relinquished all their possessions to the colony, particularly money. Nevertheless, Yos was a strong promoter of communal living upon settling in America— probably because he was a brother-in-law of Darius Walter, the senior elder of the Dariusleit. At Wolf Creek, Yos served as the school teacher.

In the early years in America, Wolf Creek Colony had serious internal problems and, although they built the community, their unresolved conflicts weakened them considerably.

More than half of the original founders eventually left the colony, opting for individual ownership. After one particularly frustrating situation, Yos left in 1877 and moved with his family and some of his friends to Bon Homme Colony. There he served as the *weinzedel* (farm manager) for eleven months. But when he was asked to commit his money to the community, he left Bon Homme also, telling the elders that he had decided to return to Wolf Creek. He very well may have, had he not stopped on the way to Wolf Creek at the home of one of his sisters, a non-communal Hutterite. Apparently, she was able to convince him that the best solution was to buy a nearby farm that was for sale. He never did return to live at Wolf Creek Colony. On September 11, 1878, he paid $1,000 for the farm, where he and his family lived for the rest of their lives. He was later selected as the minister of a small Prairieleit fellowship at Olivet, South Dakota, which met bi-weekly in private homes.

Other Hutterites didn't settle as contently. A young woman whose family had returned to communal living in a Dariusleit community, found her father in the horse barn one day, leaning against a stall. He was in tears. "What ails you, Father?" she asked. He told her he had made a terrible mistake by joining the colony. Upon moving in, he had relinquished all his belongings to the community, over which he now had very little control. He felt the leadership in the colony dealt unfairly with people, favoring certain members. "We would've done better had we not joined." he said. Nevertheless, he did stay. Today, some of his descendants live in colonies in Montana.

In the last two decades of the 19th century, the Prairieleit Hutterites gradually distanced themselves from their communal Brethren and established independent Hutterite churches in South Dakota in order to maintain their own unique brand of Hutterite faith. A hundred years ago, there were far more Prairieleit than there were communal Hutterites. They continued to think of themselves as Hutterites, representing the old traditions. Some of the early Prairieleit churches were Neu Hutterthal (rural Bridgewater), Hutterdorf (rural Freeman), Hutterthal Mennonite (rural Freeman), Bethany Mennonite (Freeman), and so on. Like other Anabaptists, they interpreted scriptures differently from the colony Hutterites. In their view, the community of goods was not biblically mandated. At first, Prairieleit preachers continued preaching the Hutterite sermons, but eventually those parts emphasizing communal living were omitted. In fact, a few preachers had already begun deleting them in Russia. The Hutterite Brethren generally considered the Prairieleit less committed to the gospel. Unlike the individualistic lifestyle of the Prairieleit, colony life demanded more cooperation, openness, group discipline, and an emphasis on simple living. The Prairieleit, they felt, had taken the easy road, and were a selfish, materialistic people.

In time, the general population assimilated most of the independent Prairieleit. In the late 1800s, Prairieleit Hutterites in South Dakota began marrying Mennonites and joining their churches. In 1884, Mennonite missionaries from Kansas converted some Prairieleit to the Krimmer Mennonite Brethren church. The name "Krimmer" came from those Mennonites who had migrated from the Ukraine to the Crimea.

Around the turn of the century, when homesteads were no longer readily available in South Dakota, some Prairieleit Hutterites immigrated to Canada and settled mostly in the Langham area of Saskatchewan. Some of these people had endured difficult times in America and were very poor. Moving to Canada and establishing themselves there set them back even further for awhile. They settled on virgin land. In the very early years they had no schools. Some children didn't go to school until they were ten or eleven years old. Before the Great Depression, virtually all Prairieleit Hutterites in the Langham area worked and lived on the farm. By then, the South Dakota Prairieleit were operating businesses in towns. During the depression, the Langham Prairieleit often talked about returning to South Dakota. But hardly anybody moved back.

It is difficult to determine the spirituality of the Langham Prairieleit and what proportion of people attended church on a regular basis and which church they belonged to. Some went to the Krimmer Mennonite Brethren Emmanuel church; others attended the Bethseda Mennonite church near Langham. The Krimmer Mennonites considered the Prairieleit to be a paganish group, hence their efforts to convert them in America.

SEATED IN FRONT: Andreas A. Stahl Sr. and wife Katherine.
STANDING IN BACK: The woman in the centre is the Stahls' daughter. The other people are the daughter's husband and children. These people stayed in the United States. Other Stahl children moved to Langham, Saskatchewan. Five of Andreas Stahl's brothers and sisters joined the Dariusleit colonies. (Photograph, around 1900—CM)

Before the Krimmer Mennonite church was established in 1917, fourteen miles northwest of Saskatoon, Prairieleit Hutterites conducted their services in the home. When their membership reached sixty people, their congregation had grown large enough to warrant the building of a church. The first Prairieleit minister of this church was Andreas A. Stahl, who had immigrated to Canada in 1901. He died in 1921, and his son A. A. Stahl Jr. took his place. In 1937, another one of Andreas Stahl's sons, Paul Stahl, was ordained to lead the congregation. Paul had spent four years training at the Moody Bible Institute in Chicago. The first congregation was later dubbed "the Stahl church."

In the summer, the Prairieleit walked to church or traveled by horse and buggy. Some went on horseback. In the winter, they traveled by bobsled. The sermons were still in High German, at first. Like their communal relatives, Prairieleit children attended Sunday school, where they memorized Bible verses and read lessons. But the Langham Prairieleit's church services were vastly different from communal Hutterites' services in at least one way. In the colonies, people sat quietly while the preacher delivered the sermon. The Prairieleit who attended the Krimmer Mennonite church would interrupt Biblical texts and hold long and sometimes heated discussions. The Krimmer

Andrew Miller (1834-1899) and his second wife, Susanna Tschetter.
(Photograph—EW)

Mennonites had lit an evangelical fervor in the people whom they converted.

There were inconsistencies, however, because some families were divided over which church to attend. Others remained detached from the church, showing up only for weddings, funerals, and other special occasions. These people preferred studying their Bibles in the home.

Culturally, the Prairieleit Hutterites maintained their uniqueness, which made them separate—or at least different—from the Mennonites and their other neighbors. Their Hutterite character continued to show in their interpersonal relationships, their warm sense of comraderie, their forthrightness, their long drawn-out visits to relatives on Sunday afternoons, their folkloric traditions, their frugality, their ethnic food, and their Hutterish language.

By the 1920s, automobiles had become more commonplace. As one Prairieleit Hutterite man told me, people didn't visit as much after that. Previously, when people went somewhere, the neighbours were often as far as they would venture. With automobiles, people became more mobile and regularly traveled further, to places such as Saskatoon.

John Z. Kleinsasser, a minister in the Bridgewater and Huron areas of South Dakota, started another Prairieleit church in Dinube, California, in 1909. Today, Prairieleit are scattered throughout the Mennonite Brethren Churches in California. They are also scattered throughout the United States and Canada.

Due to their intermarriages with people from other Christian churches, it is nearly impossible to arrive at any accurate population count for people of Prairieleit descent. In 1974, one hundred years after the first Hutterites settled in America, Prairieleit genealogist Arnold Hofer from Freeman, South Dakota, estimated that the larger population of Prairieleit (including those people with at least one Hutterite grandparent) could easily be 20,000 or more. For most of these people, the name "Prairieleit" means very little today. Some of the older people still refer to themselves as Hutterites, but most don't care to be associated with the communal Hutterites. A Prairieleit Hutterite, who grew up at Langham, informed me that most of what is written about the Prairieleit—which amounts to very little—is through the eyes of the Mennonites in South Dakota, and does not aptly describe the experience of those who migrated to Canada. My observation is this: were it not for that Mennonite influence, even less may have been written.

In the early years in America, and then more so by the second and third generations, Prairieleit Hutterites wanted to distance themselves from their relatives in the colonies. They desired association with mainstream North American culture and to be "in tune with the times." They were often embarrassed about their past, especially since they were frequently associated with the communal Brethren, with whom they had increasingly less in common. Some deplored the thought of even visiting the colonies.

In North America, the communal Hutterites practically abandoned higher education as a way to keep the world at bay. The Prairieleit criticized this. The early Hutterites were highly educated people. Some historians have even credited them as being the innovators of the institution of kindergarten in Moravia! (Today, people with Prairieleit background serve in virtually every occupation and are at every level of education. Some have also served in political office.) Prairieleit women especially disapproved of the inferior way that the colony women dressed and how they were treated in the male-dominated Hutterite communities.

Some Prairieleit in South Dakota still remember how their non-Hutterite classmates in school made fun of them, referring to them as "dirty Russians." The colony Hutterites also had derogatory terms for the Prairieleit. One man told me how insulted he felt when boys from the colony called him a "barusch," which is a derogatory term for a member of another group. It is derived from a Ukrainian word, meaning "disturber, troublesome person." In the Hutterite context it also means *agntümer* (private owners), which the Prairieleit were.

Until the 1950s, communal Hutterites often felt threatened by the Prairieleit, even to the extent of not readily welcoming them into the colonies. Contrary to what people thought, Hutterites were not wealthy. Their birthrate was still among the highest per capita in the world, therefore most of the colonies' resources went toward acquiring sufficient land and establishing new communities to accommodate their growth. There wasn't much money left after that need was met.

Some communal Hutterites were frugal to the point of embarrassment. One Prairieleit woman told me how her relative in the colony used to visit restaurants in nearby towns to collect fat scraps (ingredients for homemade soap). "Had he no pride?" she wondered. Frugality was—and still is—a Hutterite characteristic. Long before recycling was in vogue, Hutterites were recycling whatever they could. But if you add the lack of personal belongings to individual vows of poverty, it is easy to see why Hutterites would feel threatened by the Prairieleit, who, as individuals, were visibly better off. For instance, a communal Hutterite would see a new car owned by a Prairieleit person as a sign of opulence. Hutterite preachers feared that Prairieleit visiting the colonies would entice colony people to leave the community so they could obtain the same objects. As the colonies' overall wealth increased, however, these fears subsided.

In the 1940s, Prairieleit Hutterites at Langham started leaving the farm to live and work in the cities. Subsequently, they also started marrying outside of the Mennonite church. By the 1950s, the Hutterish language was no longer the first language spoken in Prairieleit homes. Young people still understood it, but spoke it with less fluency. As the older people died, so did the language.

Despite Prairieleit's general indifference toward the communal Hutterites—in 1973, a century after Hutterite delegates had come to America to look for a new homeland—Arnold Hofer from Freeman, South Dakota, along with other Prairieleit individuals, established the Hutterite Mennonite Centennial Committee. Their goal was to preserve non-communal Hutterite history, as well as commemorate a century of Hutterite life in North America. The committee's first book, *The History of the Hutterite Mennonites,* helped fill the void. Through the committee's efforts, many people came to appreciate their Hutterite heritage. Arnold Hofer has also translated numerous manuscripts, including ship lists, church history books, and diaries. Now 81, he is still involved in translating articles from German to English.

Some Prairieleit today sense they have lost much of their heritage (which is preserved to a large extent within the vibrant Hutterite communities). Most, however, wish to maintain their distance from the Hutterites. I was told that many younger descendents of Prairieleit today don't even know that their great-grandparents lived in a Hutterite community. I find it interesting, however, that more than a few colonies have hired people from Prairieleit Hutterite background as their English school teachers in the past, and continue to do so. In 1992, about twenty-two percent of the English schoolteachers teaching in Hutterite colonies understood the

Hutterish language. When I attended school at Baildon Colony, the superintendent of our school, Mr. Willms, spoke our language. I assume he was a Mennonite, with some relations to Prairieleit Hutterites. All the children loved him and looked forward to his visits.

In July, 1997, the Langham and area Prairieleit Hutterites hosted a reunion. The attendance was overwhelming. About 500 people came, some from as far away as Scotland. Another reunion is already planned for the year 2000. This suggests that some people are interested in their Hutterite heritage. I was informed that it has little to do with communal Hutterite history, though.

In 1997, Walter B. Hoover, a Prairieleit Hutterite from Saskatoon, published two important books: *The Hutterian English Dictionary* and *The Hutterian Language.* In the 470-year history of the Hutterites, someone has finally begun creating a written language from Hutterites' rich and unique oral language. Admittedly, the work isn't complete, because Mr. Hoover's work focuses primarily on the language of the Langham Prairieleit Hutterites as it was spoken around 1940, or earlier. But it does represent, in my estimation, about fifty percent of the Hutterite language.

While talking with Prairieleit Hutterites in the past few years, I asked why virtually every scholar who has written about the Hutterites has failed to include any history of the Prairieleit. Doesn't their history warrant more than just a sentence or two? From the start, I wanted to include a chapter about these people in this book. Except for the Prairieleit Hutterites in the early years in America, however, I found little in the last one hundred years of their history that sets them apart from other pioneers and mainstream North American people. Their individual histories are also very interesting, but I wanted to focus primarily on their collective history; how it relates to the Hutterites' heritage of communal living, their sojourn in different European countries, and their progressions after they abandoned communal living in the Ukraine. I am grateful that the Prairieleit whom I encountered were able to share this much with me.

I also became aware of a characteristic that explains the lack of published information about these people, particularly those who moved to Langham around the turn of the century. I realized how the early Prairieleit—like my people—had a tendency to hide their feelings from others outside their own circle. It seems that introspection into every detail of life was still a foreign concept to them—and when people migrated, they wanted to shed their past. Parents seldom talked about the "olden days" to their children. Throughout their history, Hutterites had migrated many times, always leaving their homeland, never to return. Prairieleit Hutterites wanted desperately to cut their ties with that pattern. The younger generations wanted to dress "worldly," so they wore quite stylish clothes. They wanted to look "English," to be part of that English-speaking world. In their desire to distance themselves from their past, much of their interesting history was lost. Perhaps this too can be pinned on a Hutterite characteristic. All the Hutterite chronicles were written through the prism of the Bible. Much of the cultural and secular part of our ancestors' lives is missing from the literature. When I was growing up, almost every story we were told about our ancestors was related through this prism. Yet when an older person talked about how things were in the old days—which was rare—we would listen in awe! Those early days were completely foreign to us. We were told almost nothing about our grandparents. In school we weren't taught our own secular history—it was as if it didn't exist. Apparently, no one thought it was important. The lands where our ancestors were buried were essentially foreign lands while they lived there— and more so after they left.

Some Prairieleit consider themselves neglected people because their history in the 20th century has been grossly overlooked by Hutterite scholars. Many do, after all, still consider themselves Hutterite people. And why shouldn't they? The rich Hutterite heritage is theirs also. I hope this short chapter helps put some of this Prairieleit Hutterites history into perspective.

John K. Hofer, pharmacist in Freeman, South Dakota for many years.
(Photograph—CM)

Young Prairieleit Hutterite men at Langham, Saskatchewan—about 1903. Mike Wurtz (left), Paul S. Wipf (right), and Jakob S. Wipf (front). (Photograph—EW)

**Young Prairieleit Hutterite women at Langham, Saskatchewan—about 1915.
Elizabeth Pfeifer (left) and Lydia Waldner (right).** (Photograph—CM)

Mary and Joe Waldner at Langham, Saskatchewan—about 1918.
(Photograph—CM)

TOP: Prairieleit Hutterite funeral at Langham, Saskatchewan.
(Photograph, 1920—EW)

BOTTOM: George Waldner and Katherine Wurtz at Langham, Saskatchewan.
(Photograph, early 1930s—EW)

TOP: Edna Miller (later Wurtz) with her grandmothers Anna Miller and Rebecca Hofer and her younger sister at Langham, Saskatchewan. (Photograph, 1942—EW)
BOTTOM: Left to right: Walter Hofer, Verna Waldner, Florence Waldner, and Herbert Hofer at Langham, Saskatchewan—about 1942. (Photograph—EW)

Albert and Edna Wurtz in Saskatoon, Saskatchewan (1949). Today, these Hutterites are still living on their farm near Langham, Saskatchewan. Both still speak the Hutterish language.
(Photograph—EW)

Mary Waldner (centre), visiting Dariusleit relatives at Camrose Colony, Alberta.
(Photograph, 1950—CM

LEFT: Jim "Skipper" Waldner (from South Dakota) guarding a gate at an army base near Munich, Germany, in 1958. (Photograph—EW)

Japanese Hutterites

The existence of the Owa community is an interesting and curious phenomenon. The first Japanese Hutterite community had its beginning in the mid-1950s, when Izomi Izeki, then a minister in the United Church of Christ, and ten other people sought to pattern their lives on the same biblical scriptures (Acts 2:44) as the early Hutterites did in Moravia. They established a community in Koriyama City, which has a population of 240,000 and is located about 200 kilometers north of Tokyo. All the members worked outside of the church, and their attendance fluctuated. Lacking an established communal pattern, Izeki searched for a working model for his community, visiting and studying an Israeli Kibbutz (collective farm) in 1965. However, he wasn't satisfied with this model because it did not follow the teachings of the community in the Bible.

From Japanese translations of writings by Jakob Hutter, Peter Riedemann, Andreas Ehrenpreis, and Robert Friedmann, among others, Izeki's working group learned about the Hutterites. That someone in Japan had translated numerous Hutterite writings was in itself an interesting development. It began in the 1950s, when Gan Sakakibara, a professor of social economics at a Japanese university and a layman in a Presbyterian Church, came in contact with the Mennonite Central Committee and learned about Anabaptism. In the years that followed, he immersed himself completely in Anabaptist history and doctrine, translating numerous books, mostly about the Hutterites. His first book, *Four Hundred and Fifty Years of Hutterite Martyrdom and Exile,* was published in 1967. His wife was also involved in promoting Christianity in Japan for many years, serving as president of a Christian senior high school.

In 1970, the small Japanese communal group made contact with Dariusleit Hutterites in Alberta. The Hutterites not only advised them to move out of Koriyama City, but also in 1972 donated funds to help the group purchase six acres of forest on the main island of Honshu, 140 kilometers north of Tokyo. First, Izeki's Owa community cleared the land; then, like the traditional Hutterites, the group became self-sufficient farmers, modeling their community and dress after the Dariusleit. The Japanese colony admired the traditional Hutterite garb—some even considered it high fashion. To wear a uniform is popular among many social, economic, and political groups in Japan. The Hutterites in Canada continued to donate funds to the Owa community to help them build numerous buildings, including a communal dining hall, church, and houses.

In 1977, Izeki Vetter, as they now called him (Vetter means "uncle" in the Hutterish language, but it is also used as a term of respect for older men), was ordained by the elders of the Hutterian Brethren Church at Wilson Siding Colony in Alberta. About fifteen preachers from other colonies came to witness the event. Two years later, a party of three Hutterite preachers from Canada traveled to Japan to visit the Owa community. By then the group's population was twenty-three, including children. The community is still in existence today, although its membership has not grown and is even dwindling. Whether this Hutterite colony will survive another fifty years remains to be seen.

Izomi Izeki (left) and Professor Gan Sakakibara (far right). (Photograph—LG)

The author at age nineteen, two years before leaving the colony. (Photograph, 1981—SH)

Hutterite Weggelufene

The opening scene of the 1995 documentary *Born Hutterite* showed a young man racing across the field until he reached the highway. Then a traveler from the outside world picked him up and took him from the geographical boundaries of the colony. People who leave the Hutterite way of life are called *weggelufene* or *wecchglufne* (runaways). The term likely came into usage many years ago when young men literally did run across the field to the neighbors or to the highway where a ride awaited them. These young people usually returned to the colony after a few months.

Scholars sometimes use the words "defector" and "expatriate" to describe people who leave the colonies. Both are unfortunate terms. The first one suggests a renegade or outlaw and literally means to "desert." Individuals who leave the colony have to work much harder, and often enter a far more challenging life, despite the freedoms gained. The latter term, expatriate, means "exiled" or "banished." It doesn't fit the average Hutterite weggelufener. What about "ex-Hutterite?" This term suggests that once people leave the colony they are no longer Hutterites. While they may not be Hutterites ideologically, they certainly are ethnically.

I will use the term weggelufene, but bear in mind that its scope is much broader than its literal translation. The word is generally applied to all Hutterites who leave the colony either temporarily or permanently. Its proper meaning must also include someone who "leaves home, departs from the shelter of the parents' house and community, or is assimilated by mainstream society."

Weggelufene who come home to visit are often a big influence on the next generation of youngsters. I was, too, although I always took great care not to glamorize life outside the colony. My car, which took me anywhere I wanted to go, suggested freedom of choice and good times. The truth was that my younger brothers in the colony had more "good times" than I did. In the early years I was often very lonely and insecure. I felt like a social misfit.

Leaving the colony means leaving behind the only culture a person knows: communal living. Hutterites are either *in* the colony or *out*. Leaving the colony can be compared to immigration to another country and starting a new life there. Most people plan their departure in secrecy and leave in the same way. The scene of a young man racing across the field is a bit exaggerated, yet it is also appropriate because many Hutterites do make the break by waiting for an opportune time to have someone drop them off at the nearest highway or neighbor's farm. When I left home in 1983, I waited until the adults were eating breakfast in the dining hall. With my stash of clothes under my arm, I dashed to the garages where one of the boys was warming up the 706 International tractor. Minutes later we were bumping along the gravel road leading to the highway.

Unlike many Hutterites, I left the colony with no intention of eventually returning. I had secretly converted to a different religion two years earlier. I felt that once I left home there could be no return. Spending two years in the colony with a different faith was in itself very challenging. I found myself dismantling everything the preachers were saying in church. I didn't dare tell my brothers and sisters, much less my parents or any elders, so I kept returning to books that further helped justify my findings. I visited the Moose Jaw Public Library and used bookstores whenever I could, searching for writings about esoteric matters, philosophy, and psychology. When I tried to talk about these subjects with my cousins, they were suspicious. "That psychology stuff is dangerous," some said. "If you let yourself into that, you get wrong ideas and your Hutterite faith suffers."

The truth was that my Hutterite faith consisted mostly of boundaries, colony rules, and fears of condemnation by God on Judgement

Day. The doctrine of *Gelassenheit* (surrender and service to the community) for the love of God wasn't something I understood from the heart. God and Love seemed to exist on vastly different planes. The words were certainly there in songs, prayers, and sermons, but they seemed empty against the fearsome vision I had of God, who would condemn me for having an interest in art and psychology. When I became disenchanted with the Christian religion, I believed it to be little more than a system of mind control. I have since become aware of the wider implications of this great religion and have made peace with it, although my belief in God is not based on the Bible's tenets of Original Sin and Eternal Damnation. As for the Hutterite version of Christianity, I didn't remain in the colony long enough to become fully indoctrinated into the communal faith.

This is one of the perils of living in a traditional society or growing up in an Orthodox Church. Hutterite elders are not quick to relinquish old ways out of fear of rocking the "ark" too much. Meanwhile, the world outside the colony door knocks louder and louder, penetrating the Hutterite society to such a degree that people's spirituality is threatened or impaired. Some seek a new religious experience—like I did—and leave. Not that the outside world's influence is always bad. For people living in a semi-sheltered world, however, it is often the cheap, shallow, and insubstantial characteristics of the host culture (such as depicted on television) that is most alluring. Real depth and understanding of the outside word is usually beyond a sheltered person's reach. So the young person who runs away takes all the good stuff for granted, and makes the break entirely. Some make it across to the other side successfully—others do not.

In the spring of 1983, I decided it was time to go. It took me two months to find a job. Most weggelufene secure a job before leaving. The job is the visa to their entrance into the New World. Leaving the colony is frightening, but if the weggelufener has immediate work, he or she is spared a lot of anxiety. Using the backhoe tractor, of which I was the overseer, I drove about seven times to a neighbor who lived three miles from the colony. From there I telephoned the farmers who had placed classified ads in the "Help Wanted"

section of *The Western Producer*. My "English" (non-Hutterite) clothes that I was to wear were ready. I had purchased blue jeans, shirts, and a jacket at the Salvation Army in Moose Jaw, washed them in a bucket and packed them in a small cardboard box. Nobody knew about my plans. I had dropped hints, though, hoping that it would lessen the blow to my family.

Before leaving, weggelufene go through emotional swings of fear, guilt, excitement, anticipation, and joy-filled hope. Most people keep their intent a secret because they know family and friends would try to dissuade them, complicating things even more. Someone leaving the colony to pursue a dream has a difficult time communicating this desire. Ideas of obtaining a University degree, becoming an airline pilot, or a nurse, are discouraged—even ridiculed. "What good will it do, when you lose your salvation?" is a typical response.

Most Hutterite men's first jobs outside the colony are found working on a farm or in construction, since this is where their experience has been. Women usually begin their new life as housekeepers or live-in babysitters. Many Hutterites have been taken advantage of by their first employers. A young Hutterite, who knows no other life and is used to taking orders, is often only too happy to work, glad to be away from the colony, even though he or she may be terribly homesick. More than a few teenagers have given up and returned to the colony at that stage. My first long job, as a dairy farm laborer, lasted for six months. Although the monthly wage was too low for the number of hours I worked, my employer and his family treated me well. My younger brother wasn't so lucky. He worked for a few months virtually like a slave for just room and board. Fortunately, an older cousin who had left the colony two years earlier, rescued him.

The weggelufener's departure is usually a sad affair for his family and the entire community, leaving a hole akin to someone dying. People back home are often shocked, especially if a boy had just been made overseer of a new tractor or swather, something very important to a young Hutterite. Because it's rare for women to leave Lehrerleit colonies, when two of my female cousins left Baildon in the 1980s, people were even more bereft. The colony's future looked grim.

Where would it end? Was this the beginning of women leaving the colony as was common among the Schmiedeleit?

Parents shed many tears when their children leave home. The difficulty is compounded by the Hutterites' general belief that a born Hutterite's salvation is hardly possible outside the colony. For people already baptized into the church, the break is even more severe, not only in social and physical terms but also in faith. They essentially break their baptismal vows (confession of faith) by which they promised to die a martyr's death sooner than leave the colony. Virtually all people leaving the colony after baptism do so because of a conversion to another religious experience or due to insurmountable internal conflicts.

All weggelufene's financial ties to the colony are severed, and most people leave with less than $100 in their pocket. Usually only the bare necessities such as clothes, shirts, and socks—whatever fits into a small bag or suitcase— are taken. The colony provides for individuals' welfare from the cradle to the grave, but the minute they leave, they are on their own. Families will send care packages whenever they can, but the colony is no longer responsible for the weggelufene's welfare. In 1966, the Court of Queen's Bench in Manitoba ruled that a particular family who had left their colony was not entitled to anything from back home. This family appealed the decision, but in 1970 the Supreme Court of Canada upheld the ruling. A clause in the legal constitution of the Hutterites states that people who leave the colony are not entitled to any compensation. This constitution has been challenged since, but as far as I can determine, nobody has ever been successful in obtaining any financial support after leaving the colony. It is understandable, regardless how unfair it is to the weggelufene, that the colony as a whole would seek to protect itself and its members. If one weggelufener was able to take with him some of his colony's assets, where would it end? Some colonies might soon be dismantled, financially crippled beyond repair.

Aside from being cut off financially, weggelufene lose the emotional support of their community. Church members can no longer encourage the individual because their faith and ideology forbids it. That doesn't mean that family and friends don't care. They do care, and sometimes object to strict colony rules, accommodating their departed loved ones as far as boundaries will allow. Their biggest worry is not about the weggelufener's physical needs, but rather, about his soul. They fear that helping or encouraging the weggelufener might make it easier for him to stay away and thus actually help sow the seeds of his own destruction (eternal damnation).

The fear of being desolate is often a deterrent for people who might otherwise leave the security of the colony. Weggelufene leave behind not only their family but also their friends, who sometimes feel betrayed and abandoned. During the breakup of the Schmiedeleit communities between 1989 and 1994, many people saw no other alternative but to leave the colony. Those who decided to stay were often left in situations where the factions within individual communities were unevenly divided, making it extremely difficult for some people to voice their concerns.

A runaway Hutterite's choices and translatable skills—at least when first leaving home—are quite narrow. A Hutterite man usually has more skills than a Hutterite woman for securing a job on the outside. But unless he gets some specialized training or continues his education, he will likely remain a hired hand or a common laborer all his life, receiving lower wages than what his potential might be. Inevitably, both men and women who leave the colony are required to do some catching up. Compare a twenty-one-year-old Hutterite with only a Grade 8 education to a non-Hutterite. By that age, many young people have already spent three years studying in University in order to obtain a degree. The Hutterite has received much practical, on-the-job training, and that is a bonus. However, in today's labor market, job specifications are narrowly defined and are quite complex. The Hutterite's scant academic education is a huge drawback for entrance into the skilled labor market. Hutterites can also go back to school, but the lack of financial and emotional support are deterrents many weggelufene are not able to overcome. Except for some Schmiedeleit colonies since the early 1980s, Hutterites generally grow up with less than a healthy attitude toward academic training beyond

Grade 8 or 10. This clearly shows in many weggelufene's lack of career direction and ability for long-term planning. They need role models who will inspire them to go back to school. A typical answer a weggelufener often gives for not acting quickly is: "I'll wait and see." Meanwhile the years go by.

Hutterites who do opt for higher education or specialized training to develop their careers are usually strong and focused individuals, the kind who rise to the top of their professions. My second cousin, John Wipf, is a prime example. Shortly after leaving the colony, he began studying for his high school diploma by taking correspondence school classes. He still had to support himself and kept working on the farm, studying on evenings and weekends. Later, he entered the University of Regina and earned two degrees: one in Biology, the other in Computer Science. During one semester he even achieved the status of top student at the University. Today he lives in the Philippines, developing insurance commodities for the Third World. Another cousin has his own trucking firm and operates a fleet of freight trucks in Alberta. A third cousin spent many years apprenticing in the cattle business and now has a successful career as a cattle buyer. Some young men get their start in the oil fields of Alberta and Saskatchewan. One Calgary oil company's employees are all Hutterites. Nursing is one profession many Hutterite women enter. Their training in nurturing and care-giving serves them well for this type of work after they leave the colony. Other occupations held by people that I know of are as welders, carpenters, custom crop harvesters, diamond drillers, factory workers, computer programmers, veterinarians, truck drivers, teachers, bakery owners, restaurant workers, police officers, ranchers, and farmers. The largest number of weggelufene live in or near the cities of Portage La Prairie, Brandon, Winnipeg, Lethbridge, Calgary, and Sioux Falls.

I feel that more than a few Hutterites have become better persons after leaving the colony. Their experiences outside usually challenge them to grow in areas where they previously had little concern. Also, people who return to the colony are often very anxious to take on responsibilities because life outside may have stretched them and made them more aware and appreciative of the care provided by the colony.

Hutterites abhor laziness among their own members. Likewise, healthy and able-bodied weggelufene who go on welfare programs are considered "bums"—people with no pride. Most weggelufene will avoid collecting social assistance. To do so would be admitting defeat, conceding that they can't succeed on their own.

ABOVE: The author (with hostess Gerry Peppler) promoting *The Hutterite Treasury of Recipes* **in 1987 at CKOS-CICC Television in Yorkton, Saskatchewan.** (Photograph courtesy of CKOS Television)

OPPOSITE PAGE: The author, visiting Super Print (Saskatoon) during the eighth printing of *The Hutterite Treasury of Recipes.* **By 1992, when the book was replaced by** *The Hutterite Community Cookbook,* **it had been reprinted twenty-four times.** (Photograph, 1986—WL)

Author Samuel Hofer talking with Lehrerleit German schoolteacher at Overwaitea Foods in Lethbridge, Alberta during a book signing and the filming of *Born Hutterite*. The award winning documentary was filmed and produced (1995-1996) by Black Hat Productions, in co-production with the National Film Board of Canada and the participation of Telefilm Canada. Hofer is the first professional fiction writer to emerge from the Hutterite communities. Because individual artistic pursuits are forbidden in Hutterite communities, the author left the colony in 1983. (Photograph, 1995—JW/BHP)

Thirty-five years ago, Hutterites who left the colony did so because they wanted to have fun, watch television and movies, and own money and private property. Some left to follow lifelong dreams, or to have freedom of choice and self-direction. Others left in rebellion against authority, especially when leaders showed favoritism towards their own family members. All these remain common reasons why people leave colonies today, but the major reason is religion. Since the 1970s, there has been a rapid growth in conservative Protestantism throughout North America. This religious revival not only impacted mainstream society, but also First Nations peoples

and Hutterites. The trend has created problems in quite a few Hutterite colonies. People have increasingly rejected the basic Hutterite belief—that communal living is essential for salvation—with one that emphasizes, solely, a personal relationship with Christ. No longer is it mostly young single men leaving the colonies for a few months. The problem has become more complex: girls and women, older men—occasionally even entire families—break away. It is still rare for Lehrerleit women to leave the colony, but among the Schmiedeleit, about half of the people leaving today are women. Women are less likely to return to the colony once they leave.

To some religious converts, the centuries-old Hutterite prayers, songs, and sermons provide only "head knowledge," rather than "true Christian spirit." They also consider Hutterite garb invalid for a spiritual life, seeing it merely as a tradition, having nothing to with true Christianity.

Today, Hutterites have more access to other information through radio broadcasts or print. Some are quicker to question their religion. If a preacher cannot answer their questions, members seek outside advice to help them resolve religious problems, making them vulnerable to evangelists seeking converts. More than a few Hutterites have been swayed in this way. Not only do some young people sneak away to attend movies or to watch television at a neighbor's, but also some furtively attend local gospel meetings held by traveling evangelists.

A few years ago a group of young Dariusleit people at Flat Willow Colony in Central Montana went to a nearby Evangelical Revival meeting out of curiosity. They found themselves moved by the clarity of the message, which was in English. Part of their story was told in a BBS documentary called "How to Get to Heaven in Montana." At the meeting, the message of Jesus suddenly became very clear to them. Not that the pure example isn't put forward in the Hutterite sermons. It is present—and often in the most poetic and beautiful language. However, the language barrier is insurmountable to some Hutterites. After two to three centuries, some no longer fully understand the old language. I think if the same sermons were suddenly preached in English, there would be a shakeup in the Hutterite church. That is why elders are not quick to introduce English as the language of religious instruction. It seems as though a certain amount of obscurity is necessary to hone the Hutterite faith, much of which is passed along by rote and oral tradition. During the Reformation of the 16th century, Anabaptist reformers wrote and preached in the vernacular, which helped them gain many converts. This alarmed Catholic Church leaders. Today, English more clearly represents contemporary thought and has the same effect. For that reason, the Hutterite faith depends substantially on the German language of the 17th and 18th centuries.

Often converts to another religion turn from being timid and shy to becoming bold and outspoken. Charismatic evangelism especially encourages emotional expression, which is an important part of any new religious experience. Along with this openness comes criticism towards Hutterite life. To converts, the Hutterite religion seems cold and spiritless. In the Evangelical churches, discussions and acknowledgement of personal feelings and problems are encouraged, including problems such alcoholism and drug abuse. In the colonies, problems like these are often left untreated. To people infused with a new spirit, the old methods of shunning are no longer the answer. Openness and emotional response through heartfelt prayer and personal commitment to Jesus Christ—even speaking in tongues—are considered more powerful than the old services and control systems.

"The early Hutterites," dissidents argue, "had Jesus in their confession of faith and were persecuted for their faith, not for their dress." Some critics describing the colony's system use words such as "bondage" and "spiritual death." Some openly proselytize among colony members, which creates even more problems. Elders hoping to control the situation have sometimes ceased to recognize people's membership in the Hutterite church, even though the converts still resided in the colony. For older converts, this is especially difficult. Colony life is all they know. To leave would be disastrous.

People at a crossroads, dissatisfied with life, often look to God for answers. This is when some Hutterites begin re-evaluating their faith. If exposed to another faith that promises new answers to long-held questions, a split is likely to follow. At that point, traditional doctrine loses a lot of credibility when people in leadership positions fail to exercise fairness and tact.

The new emphasis on a personal relationship with Jesus Christ is nothing new to the Hutterite faith. When you look past the highly ordered and seemingly rigid structure of the Hutterite community, you find that at the heart of the faith lies a true commitment to Jesus Christ and what He stood for in His physical life. He himself was a communal man and, according to the Bible, had no personal possessions. Whatever money Jesus had, He shared with his disciples. The ideology of communal living is paramount to such a degree in the relationship with God, however, that some critics feel Jesus Christ has taken a back seat to those traditions and old customs that serve to keep people entrenched in fear and dogma. Colony members will ostracize people who openly de-emphasize communal living as a means to salvation. They consider the dissidents to be out of control, having allowed themselves to become irrational and overwhelmed with emotion, unable to make real decisions. Most converts end up leaving, to separate from what they see as a "two-way life." One woman I talked to considered herself "an undercover Christian" while in the colony.

I have often asked myself if some of the Hutterites' quest for a new spirituality has anything to do with technological advances in the last thirty years. It is true that technology has affected the Hutterites both positively and negatively. Today, one person can feed several thousand pigs in the barn at the flick of a switch! The specialized knowledge required in certain trades often creates separation, infringing on one of the most important aspects of communal life: working together. This technology does not necessarily lead to people leaving the colony, but it slowly erodes communication and the camaraderie so characteristic of colony life thirty years ago. Elders readily admit they have a problem on their hands. "All we can do is keep the secular and spiritual in balance." one preacher said.

Not all people who leave the Hutterite colonies because of religion agree with each other. It is usually those drawn to the Evangelical charismatic movement who are most emotional and openly critical of Hutterite life. Others are more subdued and relaxed about their newfound spiritual outlook. They aren't as quick to alienate their families and other people with different religious views. In fact, some maintain close relations with the Hutterites. My friend Mary Wipf, who lives in Sioux Falls, South Dakota, left the colony more than twenty years ago due to internal community problems: her alcoholic husband and her rebellion against the colony's system of male authority over women. These problems held her in a severe state of depression for several years. Although she is still misunderstood by many of her people, including her children in the colony (who are now adults), she has maintained a good relationship with some communal Hutterites. They often come to her home when on business or during doctor visits in the city. Mary's home has been a halfway house for Hutterites, from both in and out of colonies. Her dress still has some semblance to her Hutterite past and she considers herself a Hutterite to the core. Older people, remaining true to their cultural identity, do not usually change their clothing style when they leave the colony.

Some weggelufene never make the complete transition to mainstream society. Individuals who through emigration, marriage or other influences leave their social group or culture without making the satisfactory adjustment to another, may find themselves on the margins of each while a member of neither. Encountering one of these marginal people was one reason that my older brother returned to the colony after being away for three years. He frequently saw a forty-year-old weggelufener in a bar in Coutts, Alberta. The poor chap often sat alone, talking to himself in public. Apparently, this disturbed my brother enough to make him contemplate his own future. Would he be in the same situation at age forty? Would the devil also drive him that far if he failed to return to the colony?

People on the fringes often fail to derive satisfaction from their relations with the world, becoming trapped in frustrating jobs and life situations, which they feel permit them no more freedom from outside direction than they had while in the colony. Disillusion sets in. They no longer know what they are doing outside the warm fellowship of the colony. They haven't formed any realistic long-term plan for the future. They become drifters and often find themselves *"sot"* (filled up)—even sick of the world. There is little in that world more appealing to them than what the colony offers. In all likelihood they never resolved leaving the colony and never completely closed the door to their return. These people avoid making plans for the future; they are afraid of "tying themselves down," in case they should want to return to colony life. They may have left the colony reluctantly to begin with, because of

166

community problems or favoritism by colony leaders. Adjusting to the outside world is especially hard for them.

Because of my work as a writer and publisher, the first thing people know about me is that I grew up in a Hutterite community. Many weggelufene avoid drawing attention to their Hutterite background out of fear that they will be rejected. But how can any honest and trusting friendship be developed if something so paramount as background is excluded? It is true that many non-Hutterites do have false notions about people from the colonies. This is precisely why individuals need to explain themselves. People cannot change where they are from, nor should anybody be made to look inferior because of their background. I have found openness and frankness to be the keys for sincere relations. Besides, most people do not really care that much where others are from. They have their own insecurities. Why join the crowd and perpetuate fear and misunderstanding? I decided long ago that all I could do is be the best human being I am capable of—and I hope people would want to know me for that reason and no other.

Some Hutterites who leave the colony maintain close ties with other Hutterites, even living in semi-communal situations outside the colony. My friend Tabitha, who resides in a neighborhood in Winnipeg where quite a few other weggelufene Hutterites live, is a prime example. Tabitha is a co-owner of Tall Grass Bread Company & Deli, a well-known bakery specializing in organic products. Her life is still very communal. Members of her church who arrive in Winnipeg, are encouraged to move into the area. Quite a few women who have left colonies in Manitoba have found her community and circle of friends a good place to start their new life. Some have also gained employment in her bakery. This has not weakened her relationships with colony Hutterites. Instead, it has served to strengthen them. Strong individuals somehow always manage to create an atmosphere of acceptance. Like Tabitha, these people are usually proud of their Hutterite past. It seems wherever there are women, there is usually more emphasis on community. Typically, men who leave the colony do not flock together as much, and do not wish to be part of any community of Hutterites.

In time, most weggelufene who choose not to return to communal living, drift away from their Hutterite orientation. Most people continue visiting their families in the colonies once in a while. They are not denied these privileges.

It is difficult to determine the percentage of weggelufene who eventually return to the colony, because no polls have been taken. One thing is certain: more Hutterites are leaving colonies today than did so thirty years ago. However, there are also more Hutterite colonies today. I would estimate that between seventy-five to eighty percent of weggelufene eventually return to the colony. The Hutterite way of life and religion still has a lot of appeal for most Hutterites. Weggelufene's families—unless they get married to a non-Hutterite (conversions to the Hutterite faith are rare)—never completely give up hope for their return.

Occasionally one hears of people returning to colony life even after being away for twenty or thirty years. It could be due to a midlife crisis or a realization that enslavement to the materialistic world robs them of the freedom to enjoy their spiritual life, or simply, a guilty conscience. Under these circumstances, life in the colony doesn't seem so bad after all. To the Hutterites, such a person is reason for celebration. The weggelufener has won the fight against the devil and, like the prodigal son, has come home.

Frequently Asked Questions and Misconceptions about Hutterites

I sometimes am invited to read and speak in libraries and schools. This is when I get a chance to personally respond to questions Canadians have about Hutterites. Many people have stereotypical views and are poorly informed. Hutterites are partly to blame because, until recently, they have not gone out of their way to explain themselves to the general public. Consequently, they have been perceived as arrogant and aloof. Most Hutterites believe that their lifestyle, based on what they see as principles of the early Christian church, is witness enough for the outside world. Also, the average Hutterite does not have the English language skills to articulate his or her lifestyle and faith other than through a few clichéd homilies, which often serve only to perpetuate stereotypes. I hope that the push for higher education in some colonies will change that.

Hutterites *do* care about how the world sees them. Elders have usually been open to speak to journalists and sociologists. The problem with newspaper articles is that they deal with surface material only and are terribly repetitive. Scholarly theses are seldom conclusive; the researcher must wade through a great amount of material, then live among the Hutterites for awhile. Otherwise, the so-called new material is mostly a rehash of previous studies.

I have tried to incorporate an abundance of details about Hutterite life into this book. I hope by now you have a better understanding of the Hutterites. But I am assuming you still want to know more. Here are the questions people most frequently ask me, as well as the most common misconceptions about the Hutterites. I have carefully answered each one.

Are Hutterites Christians?

Yes. Hutterites are a Christian sect belonging to the Anabaptist branch of Christianity. And they are—in theory and practice—some of the most devout Christians on the planet. One of the fundamentals of the Hutterite faith is literal interpretation of the Bible, which includes an unshakeable belief in Jesus Christ. Hutterites celebrate more Christian holidays than most Christians do. They celebrate Christmas, Good Friday, Easter, the Resurrection, Ascension Day, Pentecost—even New Years Day is a kind of religious holiday. Hutterites attend a church service every evening of the week and another on Sunday mornings. Children eight years of age and up, young adults, and adults not yet baptized also attend Sunday school in the afternoon of every Sunday of the year and every religious holiday. Kindergarten and German school consist mostly of learning Christian principles, as well as memorizing scriptures, songs with a Christian message, prayers, and so on.

Despite all this, there are people—particularly members of Evangelical churches and those who have left the Hutterite faith and joined non-denominational congregations emphasizing rebirth in Christ—who do not consider Hutterites to be Christians. "The Hutterites," they argue, "are like the Catholics with their many saints. They are more concerned about maintaining traditions than having a relationship with Jesus Christ." This is an unfair generalization, because it is difficult to separate Hutterite life from actual beliefs of individuals. For Hutterites, living in community is living their faith. Nevertheless, some Hutterites are quick to point out that other church members, due to their "unchristian-like" actions, are not true Christians. Communal life is all that most Hutterites know, therefore some never really get challenged in ways they would be if they were on their own. For some individuals, this lifestyle is merely a convenience.

Isn't Communism the same thing as Hutterite communal life?

Socialism based on the theories of the political philosophers Karl Marx and Friedrich Engels, emphasizing common ownership of the means of production and a planned economy, is politically driven. Hutterianism, although it also emphasizes common ownership, is based on religion. Communism is based on the theory that religion is the opiate of the people. Hutterites believe that Christian beliefs and practices are necessary for salvation. There are certain expectations and conditions members in the colony must meet, but these are voluntary. Unlike Communism, in Hutterianism nobody becomes a member due to force or compulsion. There is social pressure, no doubt, but that cannot be compared to the military pressure of Communist countries. Another important difference between Communism and Hutterite communal life is that each colony operates independently in a decentralized fashion both politically and economically. If a colony fails because of poor management, the whole fellowship is not jeopardized. Colonies experiencing financial difficulties are helped out by other colonies, but not all business practices (which may be experimental in nature) are automatically applied to the rest of the colonies. This arrangement is not at all like the old Soviet collective farm system.

Other communal societies such as Shakers, Doukhobors, Harmonists, and the Amanas existed at one time. What is the secret of the Hutterites' longevity?

If you ask a devout Hutterite, he or she will likely tell you that the faith is built upon an unshakeable foundation of true community initiated 2000 years ago by Jesus Christ; after His ascent to heaven, the Son of God sent the Holy Spirit to establish the communal church through the Apostles. A devout Hutterite will also remind you that many hundreds of forebears gave their lives for this faith, and in so doing they laid the foundation—and it is by the Grace of God that their suffering has not been in vain.

I think the Hutterites' survival can also be attributed to other factors. In Moravia, they effectively eliminated the feudal system for its members by living communally. This won over many converts. Because of heavy persecution in Europe, they had to flee several times to other countries and start anew. This made them a vigilant people. Because they were isolated in what were to them essentially foreign countries, they learned to be dependent on each other as a group. Throughout most of their history, particularly in North America, Hutterites have been able not only to manage and control change, but also to maintain a distance between themselves and the rest of society. Hutterites are encouraged to rely on their leaders and the traditional interpretation of doctrine. This is why change is always a conscious decision on the part of church leaders, rather than an individual innovation.

Why do they dress that way?

Garb has always been important to Hutterites because it helps them achieve a certain distance from mainstream society through their appearance. Their clothing is an adaptation of their peasant ancestors' dress. It speaks volumes about their origins and their resistance to worldly influence. In theory, their garb makes them a plain people, holding to the belief that ornaments and finery are contrary to biblical principles. By wearing clothes in a consistent pattern, Hutterites are always conscious of being outwardly identified as Christians. Women wear kerchiefs as admonished by Saint Paul, who wrote that women in prayer should wear a head covering. Since Hutterites are considered to be in prayer at all times by virtue of their lifestyle, women always wear kerchiefs outside the home. Men wear black clothing because it symbolizes solemnity, humility, and plainness. As fashions evolved in the last two centuries, the Hutterites and other so-called plain people maintained their nonconformity through their dress. Not all details of Hutterite dress are matters of doctrine, but rather a means of expressing and maintaining scriptural teachings on modesty, simplicity, and separation.

But what do cowboy hats, colorful dresses, and polka-dot kerchiefs have to do with Christian solemnity, humility, and plainness? Good question! People in general often dress to proclaim their ethnic, social, economic, or workplace identity. Hutterite garb has evolved. It also has something to do with the evolution of ethnicity, not just separation. Separation is still important for elders, but I doubt that the average Hutterite—much less, young people—dress that way because they wish to convey their uniqueness to the world. If not constrained by their society's rules, many young Hutterites would abandon their style of dress very quickly. Another advantage that Hutterite garb achieves is that it becomes difficult to form different social classes within the Leit. There is virtually no distinction in that regard.

Ironically, Hutterites are very fashion conscious. There is a constant evolution going on within each Leit: people push the boundaries of what is accepted by the elders. Businesses such as June's Fabrics in Lethbridge have a vibrant enterprise selling to the Hutterites. The *schneider* (head tailor) of each colony orders a tremendous amount of fabric; Hutterite women manufacture virtually all their clothes themselves. Women frequently trade material with relatives from other colonies and compete with each other over who can be the first to wear a certain dress fabric in their home colony.

I've heard that because of inbreeding problems, Hutterites hire non-Hutterite men to impregnate women from the colonies in order to get new blood into their communities. Is this true?

This outrageous myth has been around for many years. To show how persistent and insidious it is; in 1993 a widely-known Hutterite scholar (whose name I won't mention) asked me the same question. This person spent many years studying the Hutterites, and even lived with them for several months. Yet even he wasn't sure what to

believe anymore. A businessman from Saskatchewan had told this scholar that the elders of one colony had propositioned him to perform the service. Newspaper advertisements have even been found, asking for "studs." In an article published in the *Brandon Sun* in 1983, Edward Boldt, a University of Manitoba sociologist, stated that he had tracked down several such ads. "Not one was placed by a Hutterite," he said. "It's usually someone playing a prank, or looking to discredit the Hutterites."

What about people who insist that they know someone who has been propositioned by the elders of a colony to do the act for $50 or a $100? I have noticed a consistent pattern there also. Seldom will you actually meet the person who was propositioned. It is the old "friend of a friend" routine. When challenged to prove it, nobody has ever been able to come up with any proof. A cousin of mine (who left the colony and who dresses in mainstream Canadian fashion) met a young patron in a Moose Jaw bar; the man claimed to have been a sperm donor to a Hutterite colony and said he was paid $100. My cousin challenged him for proof. Backed into a corner, after my cousin revealed his identity, the man admitted he was lying.

The myth is even more absurd when you consider how Hutterites actually view sexual relations. According to Hutterite doctrine, sex outside of a marital relationship is a horrific sin, punishable (if a person is baptized or married) by *aus shlus* (shunning or banning). Shunning is temporary ex-communication from the Hutterite church. During this time a member is avoided socially and not referred to as a brother or sister of the church. The shunned person is believed to be without the covenant of the church; should he or she be so unfortunate as to die at this time, salvation may not be possible. This is the "ban" which the Hutterites believe is taught in Romans 16:17; 1 Corinthians 5:9-13; 2 Thessalonians 3:6-14; 2 Timothy 3:2-5, and Titus 3:10. Whether you agree or disagree with such a drastic religious rule, it does reveal how absurd the sperm donor myth is.

Here's one more inconsistency: Since the early 1990s, some colonies have requested that weggelufene get tested for HIV upon returning to the colony. Would the Hutterites, who are very clean, orderly, and religious people, be so naïve as to hire just anybody off the street for $100 and put their lives and colony at risk?

Clearly, this myth was born out of ignorance and racism.

How are the three Hutterite groups different from each other?

Although the three groups share a common body of beliefs, language, and social customs, there are variations in dress, appearance, and character.

The most obvious differences are in their dress and appearance. Dariusleit women's dress colors are usually darker than the other Leit's. Lehrerleit women's kerchiefs have larger polka dots. Some Dariusleit women's kerchiefs have no polka dots at all. Schmiedeleit women's fashions are less consistent, they generally don't wear aprons, and their kerchiefs don't cover their hair as fully.

On the whole, the Lehrerleit are the most conservative. Their elders usually think matters through more thoroughly than the other groups do. As a result, there is more consistency from one colony to the other and they are more successful in keeping old traditions alive. The Schmiedeleit are usually more open to worldly influences. This clearly shows in their progressiveness in English school education and their desire to make the union with the Society of Brothers work in the 1970s and 1980s. Schmiedeleit are also more involved in enterprises not directly related to agriculture, namely manufacturing. This is in part due to their land holdings being smaller than the other groups'.

The Dariusleit are somewhere in the middle. On the whole, they are not as conservative as the Lehrerleit, yet not as liberal minded as the Schmiedeleit.

Why don't the groups intermarry?

In recent years, a few marriages have occurred between Dariusleit and Schmiedeleit. Maybe this is the beginning of a trend. In the early years in America, the Hutterites had many internal problems. The Schmiedeleit and Dariusleit had intended to form one group upon settling in America, but they were not able to overcome their differences. The Lehrerleit, who came three years later, were often the mediators between the groups. At first, people from all three groups intermarried, but their differences were severe enough to keep them from forming one Leit. Hutterites are a very clannish people. The Hutterites in South Dakota had many prejudices about other groups. Gradually, they drifted further apart. When they immigrated to Canada in 1918, the Schmiedeleit settled in Manitoba and the Dariusleit and Lehrerleit moved to Alberta. The distance served to separate the Schmiedeleit from the other groups even further.

If the groups don't intermarry regularly, and they have very few converts, don't Hutterites have problems with inbreeding?

Geneticists have done several studies in this area. Obviously, there are some concerns. However, I have not been able to find enough conclusive published evidence to determine that Hutterites have a huge problem with inbreeding. They don't seem to have more health problems than any other people do.

If Hutterites are so religious, why do they allow alcohol consumption?

Most Christians do not consider alcohol consumption to be sinful. Neither do Hutterites— as long as alcohol is consumed in moderation. When a member of the church does get intoxicated, it becomes a sin (lust of the flesh), and he or she is required to make a confession to the minister in order to be reprimanded and counseled by the brethren.

Hutterites make excellent wines that rival those you can buy commercially. Rhubarb wine, dandelion wine, raisin wine, and chokecherry wine are their specialties. Winemaking is one of the financial manager's official badges of office. Most colonies allot at least a half-gallon to each adult every month. Do some Hutterites drink too much? Yes. Where there is alcohol, there are alcoholics. In some colonies, alcoholism is a problem. Some Hutterites purchase alcohol themselves from liquor stores, and some frequent pubs in towns and cities. This is not to say there is anything intrinsically wrong with purchasing alcohol or going into the bar. The problem with alcohol abuse in colonies is made worse by individuals needing to moonlight for private money in order to support their habit. Sadly, livestock managers are often offered kickbacks by feed salespeople—or they ask for it—in booze or coin. The tip money isn't necessarily spent on alcohol, but far too often it is. In my view, if booze is involved, both parties are guilty of unethical business practices. Some Hutterites will deny that there is an alcohol problem in *their* colony, when indeed there is. "We know some colonies have a problem with that," they say, "but we don't." These people are in denial. Their problems will not go away.

What happens if an unmarried girl or woman gets pregnant in the colony?

Thirty years ago, pregnancies among teenagers or unmarried young Hutterites were rare. Today, inhibitions are more relaxed among young people. Pregnancies out of wedlock do occur even in colonies. A few individuals who are not yet baptized—both women and men—are known to be sexually active. Nowadays, young adults in Hutterite colonies have more access to magazines, radio and television. The sexual images portrayed through these mediums are very powerful. Furthermore, the spacious and modern unit-houses in most colonies provide more privacy than the old-style houses of the past. Unless the parents of the illegitimate child are cousins, they must get married. This is true for Lehrerleit; the Schmiedeleit and Dariusleit are more relaxed about it. I have heard of cousins (couples) who left the colony, had a child or two, then returned, hoping the community would allow them to get married. This ploy has never worked. Hutterites abide by Canadian Law, which prohibits first cousins to get married, but they do allow second cousins to wed.

Are adoptions allowed?

I have heard of some Schmiedeleit couples who have adopted children born to non-Hutterite parents, but I do not know of any Lehrerleit or Dariusleit having adopted a child from a non-Hutterite mother. One woman I know of had twins, so she gave her next child (a girl) to her sister to raise. If a couple is infertile, it is thought to be God's will. Hutterites consider children to be gifts from God, and so they are wanted. A child's welfare is insured by the whole community, therefore the typical reason for adoption (the parents not being able to provide for the child) is not a factor. In another case I know of, which occurred about fifty years ago, an older man, known to be a womanizer, raped a teenage girl. She became pregnant. Shortly after the baby was born, the girl's father took the child to the wife of the culprit and asked that she and her husband raise the child. They complied. Unfortunately, Hutterite communities are not immune to these kinds of problems. Generally, they prefer dealing with the problems themselves.

Is birth control allowed in the colony?

Officially, birth control is forbidden. Hutterites heed the admonition in Scriptures: "Be ye fruitful and multiply" (Gen. 1:28). Until about 1965, Hutterites followed that order to the letter. Their fertility rate was among the highest in the world, if not the highest. Some families had as many as fifteen children. An average family had ten children. Then came a dramatic decline in the number of births per family, a trend that continues to date. If birth control is not allowed, how does one explain that?

"Here's how it works," a man might explain, jokingly, although his answer does go to the heart of the matter. "It has to do with economics. Today, with all the big equipment we use, having too many men on a colony just isn't good. People need jobs. If people don't have work, they get into the wrong kind of work—for their own pocket. With all the land required these days for farming, and capital needed to build the modern houses, barns and operations, it can cost up to fourteen million dollars to establish a new colony. These days there are fewer resources for purchasing land for new colony expansion and this somehow indirectly effects fertility."

Here is another man's humorous explanation: "The modern family units today have basements, which means there is more room, enabling Hutterite men to sleep alone more often." A woman might say very little and avoid the subject altogether. If pressed, she might say in a roundabout way: "Today, women just aren't as strong as they used to be. By the time a woman has six or seven children, her health is in pretty rough shape. With advice and assistance from the family doctor, this problem is remedied so the woman's health doesn't deteriorate completely."

The question really ought to be: Do Hutterites practice birth control? The truth is that economics, environment, family, and community all converge—and people adapt accordingly. The only satisfactory explanation for the dramatic decline in Hutterite fertility is that the women themselves are terminating their child-bearing years much earlier these days. In some cases, contraceptions are allowed if suggested by a doctor, or if permission is given by the colony preacher (when a woman has too many children already). Another factor worth considering in explaining the lower birth rate today is that Hutterites often wait until their mid-twenties—or even later—to get married, as opposed to age nineteen, which was the common age for marriage thirty or forty years ago. Naturally, this reduces a woman's childbearing years.

Are Hutterite Marriages Arranged?

No. But apparently, earlier in Hutterites' history, there were arranged marriages. Courtship and romance scarcely existed back then. A married man referred to his wife as *eheliche schwester* (married sister), emphasizing membership in the church. Those wishing to get married informed the elders, and when the appointed time came—usually in the spring or fall—they were called to one of the bruderhofs (colonies), where the elders did the matching. Many of the prospective couples had never met each other. After a service, the young men and women were lined up on opposite sides of the room. A man had a choice of three women. A woman could refuse, but that meant she wasn't eligible for marriage until the next matching session about six months later. The matching procedure was followed by the wedding.

People weren't always happy with these marriage arrangements, yet the tradition remained in effect until about 1830, when the Hutterites were living near the Mennonites in the Molotchna district of the Ukraine under the council of Johann Cornies, a Mennonite trustee of the government. A young woman, compelled to marry an older widower whom she did not want, refused to do so. She escaped and appealed to Johann Cornies, who immediately transferred her to a distant Mennonite farm. In the meantime, he convinced the Hutterite elders to abandon the old ways, allowing eligible women to express consent to the proposed marriages.

After this episode, relatives still exerted their influence and often even arranged a partner, but it was accepted only if both parties agreed to the marriage. Today, these traditions are long gone: young people court each other. There are usually plenty of intercolony visits, giving young people opportunities to meet and begin relationships.

In reading your *Born Hutterite* stories, I was surprised to learn that Hutterite children are strapped or "whipped" for breaking rules, or for simply misbehaving. This seems so unlike pacifist people.

For Hutterites, pacifism has less to do with corporal punishment than with the faith of non-resistance in the event of war. Hutterites follow the Bible literally—the age-old admonishment to parents that to spare the rod is to spoil the child. This is interpreted as disciplining by strap or switch, if necessary. Generally, the parents and the German schoolteacher are the ones responsible for disciplining the children. Seldom does punishment come from another member of the community. It would not be accepted. People would rebel. In some colonies, the German schoolteachers no longer strap children other than their own. In recent years, individuals who left the colony as adults have filed complaints, reporting to the police that they experienced abuse at the hands of the German teacher. So teachers are acting more cautious. Instead of receiving a strapping, a child is sent to the schoolhouse after school to sit alone for a while.

Hutterites have accumulated inestimable wealth because they do not pay their fair share of taxes.

Hutterites lost their religious tax exemption in 1961. The colonies pay taxes as trust. They hand over taxes on net income divided among all colony workers over the age of eighteen, even though individuals join the community's labor force at age fifteen. Hutterites also expend tax money twice for education. They submit full property taxes in addition to funding their own schools. Because Hutterite schools are located on colony grounds, children do not require transportation to schools, yet each colony must pay the education tax. Here is what the *Brandon Sun* related in an article on May 4, 1983, after interviewing Dave Morris, the accountant for many Hutterite colonies in Manitoba: "They (the Hutterites) fall under a special section of the Income Tax Act which allows them to make a deemed allocation of the colony's income to each member, and pay taxes accordingly. Because of their special status they don't qualify for the same advantages available to farm corporations, nor can they split the family income, an advantage that recently became available to family farms." In the final tally, the Hutterites probably pay more taxes than most other farmers do.

In 1990, Saskatchewan's Hutterite colonies donated $50,000 to the University of Saskatchewan's agricultural college building fund. Agricultural research is very important to Hutterites. "We feel we owe it," a Hutterite elder was quoted in the Leader Post. "They (the college) are doing a lot for farmers." In the end, it all balances out. There is no free lunch for anybody.

Hutterites have an unfair advantage because they don't have to pay labor costs.

True, Hutterites do not pay wages to their people. I can understand the small businessperson's point. I don't think Hutterites should be singled out. When a few colonies in Manitoba started manufacturing enterprises a few years ago, people working in this area also began complaining. It seems as though the Hutterites can't make a single move without somebody begrudging their success. This is a free country. Hutterites abide by the same laws of the Charter of Rights and Freedoms. I don't think they are really upsetting the local economy because their members are not paid any wages. Hutterites do operate on a very different economy of scale than most businesses and corporations. Individual colonies are not getting wealthy beyond their means. Hutterites also have living costs. Individuals in the colony have all their needs met by the community from the cradle to the grave. Certainly this kind of security is worth something to individuals and families—and it costs something too.

Hutterites don't contribute to the local economy.

Often, a colony's requirements for goods are beyond the inventory of rural stores. They do shop around for the best prices and the larger centers usually win. Most prudent business people do that. Just look at the full parking lots and the long line-ups at Costco Wholesale. Why should Hutterites be any different? Still, the colonies do buy a tremendous amount of commodities locally. John Ryan, an Associate Professor of Geography at the University of Manitoba and author of *The Agricultural Economy of Manitoba Hutterite Colonies,* spent several years studying the economy of the Hutterites. In 1977, Dr. Ryan found that eighty percent of the Hutterites' farm machinery was purchased within a forty-kilometer radius of a given colony. Purchases of fuel, grease, fertilizer, farm chemicals, and lumber were also made locally. As a bookseller since 1986, I have traveled, sometimes more than once a year, to almost every village and town that has a Hutterite community nearby. I have seen Hutterites shopping in local drugstores, grocery stores, hardware stores, and elsewhere. While individual Hutterites may not spend as much money in these establishments as other local people do, they nevertheless are valued as customers by many retailers. In reality, Hutterites colonies are no greater threat to a community's economy than are large family farms.

Hutterites don't contribute to the local fabric of society.

It is true that Hutterites do not usually support local community centres, theaters, arts groups, and other organizations that are crucial for social and cultural interaction. From an outsider's perspective, this *is* a definite minus. However, to say that Hutterites don't contribute at all to the local fabric of society is an unfair generalization. For example, Hutterites often help poverty-stricken families with food and clothing, and donate in coin to hospitals and local charities. At blood-donating time, Hutterites go by the van or truckload. On more than one occasion I have heard of Hutterites donating their time, equipment, and labor force to pave the streets of a local town or to perform other similar jobs for the community. It is not unusual to see Hutterites helping during floods and fires, clearing their neighbors' roads of snow in the winter, or helping them with their seeding or harvesting. Many people in towns and villages near colonies do have Hutterite friends, and there are many visits back and forth. I have met hundreds of people whose Hutterite neighbors are very dear to them. One woman and her daughters even considered their Hutterite friends as family, referring to a certain older Hutterite woman as "Grandma." Others have told me their lives have been enriched immeasurably by their Hutterite neighbors, that these people are the kindest and most generous people they have ever known. Usually, people concerned about a Hutterite colony moving into their area soon find that their fears were unfounded. I am not suggesting that the reverse is never true. I am merely pointing out that it is unfair to attach labels and to paint every Hutterite colony with the same harsh brush.

What about culture? Isn't the fabric of society immensely enriched by the many different cultures in North America? Haven't people throughout history learned to become more tolerant of other societies precisely because they had them in their midst? What about the principles of community and the model of efficiency that the Hutterites stand for? Don't these have some positive spin-offs? Wouldn't it be more useful to try to learn from the Hutterites co-operative system of farming than to constantly find ways to gripe about them? Isn't the social fabric of the country enriched because we have a minority like the Hutterites in our midst? They are far from perfect, as I have indicated. But their relatively simple and peaceful ways are an alternative to the difficulties that plague many communities in North America today. I am not being sentimental here. Hutterites, too, have challenges. I believe that if people look for positive aspects, they will always find them.

Hutterites are hungry for more land and push land prices beyond the reach of other buyers.

On November 28, 1987, *The Globe and Mail* published an article about the efforts of the Saskatchewan Association of Rural Municipalities to again control Hutterite expansion. This time the association wanted to legislate that colonies be at least eighty kilometers from one another. A director of the association was quoted: "The Hutterites are taking advantage of the declining price of prairie farmland." One year the Hutterites are blamed for paying too much for land because they have the ability to pay for it! Then the next year they're blamed for buying the land when the prices have come down! What are they supposed to do? If Hutterites were in the market for buying houses in city suburbs, rest assured that some people would be complaining about that, too. People who oppose Hutterites hardly ever seem to consider that markets fluctuate. People buy at opportune times or when they need to buy. Yes, Hutterites do have the ability to pay high prices for land, but so do other large corporate farmers. The total amount of land owned by Hutterites in North America is small compared to that of other corporate farms. For the most part, theories that Hutterites are responsible for rural depopulation are unfounded. Yet I can see a farmer's dilemma, trying to hang onto the family farm. We all have much to lose if our small farms go. However, singling out a visible minority without offering solid evidence, does not do justice to human society.

In a recent conversation with someone from southern Saskatchewan, I was told of one individual in the Swift Current area who tried to convince the people in his locality to block the sale of land to a Hutterite community. This man was considered a "liberal thinker," possessing a great deal of tolerance for people of other cultures. Already a large corporate farmer, he too had his eyes on the land when it came up for sale. When he realized that a Hutterite colony had also put in a bid, his liberal and tolerant attitudes suddenly changed. What is one to make of that? People who oppose the Hutterites often have ulterior motives. I am not suggesting that some people don't have legitimate concerns. Not all Hutterite colonies are considerate enough of their neighbors. They, too, need to be constantly re-educated. But 300 municipalities in Saskatchewan ganging up on a minority group in order to legislate that they settle no less than eighty kilometers of each other is alarming.

Here are some more facts: As soon as a Hutterite colony is established and has paid its debts, it must accumulate reserves for building a new colony. A colony branches out every sixteen to twenty years. They have, by their very nature of rapid expansion, always been literally driven to efficiency. However, in Manitoba, colonies have reduced their land holdings in the last twenty years. High land prices take a big bite out of cash reserves, so some colonies have started other enterprises such as feed manufacturing, rafter building, and hog barn equipment fabrication, among others. Some of these ventures bring tremendous social challenges to the colonies, since Hutterites must meet the demands of these new businesses. Hutterites aren't immune to changes in the market place. While people struggle to keep their family farm, Hutterites struggle to keep their communities intact. Competence in the market place has nothing to do with someone's religion— although quite often, good values will go a long way.

The small farmer does have to compete in the marketplace whether there are Hutterites around or not. Economics and demographics are always changing. Dependence on a single commodity is no longer realistic in today's farm economy, unless the producer invests in massive proportions. Diversification and multiple streams of income are the keys. Hutterites do not force people to sell their farms and move off the land. History has taught this religious group that its communities run most efficiently with fewer than 130 people per colony. After surviving legislation and restrictions on land holdings in the past, which discriminated against them, Hutterites are working very closely with government liaison committees. These ensure that strict guidelines are followed so as not to box in the property of individual farmers, and so that a colony's construction displaces as few school children as possible. Although Hutterites are without doubt the beneficiaries of the technological advancements of agriculture and the evolution of the large corporate farm, who has the right to hold it against them?

And here are a few statistics: Through his research in the 1970s, John Ryan found that, although the Hutterites made up 4.5 percent of the Manitoba farm population, they owned only 1.3 percent of the farmland. Yet with their mixed farming economy, they produced approximately a quarter of the eggs and turkeys in Manitoba, as well as ninety percent of the geese! In 1973, Hutterites owned 1.1 percent of arable land in the provinces where they reside. In 1982, they owned 1.75 percent, only a fraction more. In 1981, Hutterites formed 3.6 percent of the total farm population in all of Saskatchewan, Alberta and Manitoba. Yet, Hutterite farmland still accounted for only 1.3 percent of prairie farmland. These are signs of efficiency and smart planning. Maybe others can learn from the Hutterite model.

Bibliography

Books and Theses

- Bainton, Roland H., *The Age Of The Reformation.* NJ: D.Van Nostrand Company, Inc., Princeton, 1956.
- Brewer, Cobham E., *The Dictionary of Phrase & Fable.* Blitz Editions, Leicester, 1990.
- Friedmann, Robert., *The Epistles of the Hutterian Brethren.* IN: Mennonite Quarterly Review, Goshen, 1946.
- Friedmann, Robert., *Hutterite Preaching and Worship.* IN: Mennonite Quarterly Review, Goshen, 1966.
- Friedmann, Robert., *Hutterite Studies.* IN: Mennonite Historical Society, Goshen, 1961.
- Garraty, John A. (ed.) and Gay, Peter (ed.).; *The Columbia History of the World.* NY: Harper & Row Publishers, New York, 1972.
- Goertz, Reubon., *Princes, Potentates, and Plain People: The Saga of the Germans from Russia.* SD: The Center For Western Studies, Sioux Falls, 1994.
- Gross, Leonard., *The Golden Years Of The Hutterites.* PA: Herald Press, Scottdale, 1980.
- Gross, Paul S., *The Hutterite Way.* SK: Freeman Publishing Co. Ltd., Saskatoon, 1965.
- Hofer, Yos., *The Diaries of Joseph ~Yos~ Hofer.* (translated from German by Arnold M. Hofer). SD: Hutterite Mennonite Centennial Committee, Freeman, 1997.
- Hofer, Joshua., *Japanische Hutterer: Ein Besuch bei der Owa Gemeinde.* MB: James Valley Book Center, Elie, 1985.
- Hofer, Samuel., *The Hutterite Community Cookbook.* SK: Hofer Publishers, Saskatoon, 1992.
- Hofer, Samuel., *Born Hutterite.* SK: Hofer Publishers, Saskatoon, 1991.
- Hofer, John., *The History Of The Hutterites.* MB: James Valley Colony, 1988.
- Holzach, Michael., *The Forgotten People* (translated from the German by Stephan Lhotsky). SD: Ex Machina Publishing Co., Sioux Falls, 1993.
- Hoover, Walter B., *The Hutterian Language – A grammar and lexicon.* SK: Saskatoon, 1997
- Hoover, Walter B., *Hutterian-English Dictionary.* SK: Saskatoon, 1997.
- Horsch, John., *Hutterite Brethren (1528-1931) A Story of Martyrdom and Loyalty.* IN: Mennonite Historical Society, Goshen, 1931.
- Hostetler, John A., *Hutterite Society.* M.D: John Hopkins University Press, Baltimore, 1974.
- Hostetler, John A., *Hutterite Life.* PA: Herald Press, Scottdale, 1983.
- Hutter, Jakob., *Brotherly Faithfulness: Epistles From A Time Of Persecution.* NY: Plough Publishing House, Rifton, 1979.
- Janzen, Rod A., *Perceptions of the South Dakota Hutterites in the 1980s.* SD: Freeman Publishing Co., Freeman, 1984.
- Kant, Joanita., *The Hutterite Community Cookbook.* PA: Good Books, Intercourse, 1990.
- Konker, Claudia Sue., *Conceptions Of Child Abuse: A Micro And Macro Perspective.* University of Washington, 1992.
- Miller, Levi., *Our People: The Amish and Mennonites of Ohio.* PA: Herald Press, Scottdale, 1992.
- Peter, Karl A., *The Dynamics of Hutterite Society.* AB: The University of Alberta Press, Edmonton, 1987.
- Peter, Victor., *All Things Common.* MN: The University of Minnesota Press, Minneapolis, 1965.
- Ryan, John., *The Agricultural Economy of Manitoba Hutterite Colonies.* McClelland and Stewart Ltd., Toronto. 1977.
- Scheer, Herfried., *Die Deutsche Mundart der Hutterischen Brüder in Nordamerika.* Verband der wissenschaftlichen Gesellschaften Österreichs, 1987.
- Scott, Stephen., *Why Do They Dress That Way?* PA: Good Books, Intercourse, 1986.
- Stonequest, Everett V., *The Marginal Man: A study in Personality and Culture Conflict.* NY: Charles Scribner's Sons, New York, 1937.

- *The Chronicles Of The Hutterian Brethren.* (translated and edited by the Hutterian Brethren). NY: Plough Publishing House, Rifton, 1987.
- *The History Of The Hutterite Mennonites.* SD: Hutterite Mennonite Centennial, Freeman, 1974.
- *Treasures of Time – Chapter XVIII, The Hutterian Brethren.* MB: RM. of Cartier, Elie, 1985.
- Waldner, Tony., *History of Forest River Community.* ND: Forest River Community, Fordville, 1990.
- Waltner, Emil J., *Banished For Faith.* ARK: End Time Handmaidens, Inc., Jasper, 1968.
- Youmans, Vance Joseph., *The Plough And The Pen –Paul S. Gross and the Establishment of the Spokane Hutterian Brethren.* NC: Parkway Publishers, Boone, 1995.
- Ziegelschmid, AJF. (ed.)., *Das Kleingeshichtbuch der Hutterischen Brüder.* NY: Carl Schurz Memorial Foundation, Philadelphia, Penn. and Ithaca, 1947.

Articles

- "Accepting a hard life: Hutterites a world unto themselves." The Regina Leader Post, Sept. 8, 1989.
- "Age, Gender, and Influence in Hutterite Colonies." Gertrude Enders Huntington, Communities, Spring, 1996.
- "Alberta Commission Studying Problem of Hutterite Land." The Saskatoon Star Phoenix, February 10, 1947.
- "All Things in Common?: The Contingent Nature of Communalism Among the Hutterites." Jeff Longhofer, Journal of Mennonite Studies, Vol. 11, 1993.
- "Archipelago Of Faith." Laura Rance, Brandon Sun, May 4, 1983.
- "Folklore and Ethnicity: 400 Years of Hutterite Hymnsinging." Diana M. Rankin, AHSGR Journal, Fall, 1981.
- "Group eyes own school boards." Catherine Mitchell, Winnipeg Free Press, June 26, 1996.
- "Hutterites donate money to U of S." The Regina Leader Post, February 1, 1990.
- "Hutterites Flock To School." Catherine Mitchell, Winnipeg Free Press, May 24, 1996.
- "Hutterites in Alberta." Carolyn Abraham, The Calgary Herald, October 13, 1997
- "Hutterites' rule upheld: Disobedient member loses bid to overturn expulsion." Aldo Santin, Winnipeg Free Press, November 1, 1989.
- "Is communal living a right?" Terry Johnson, Alberta Report, February 13, 1989.
- "Jacob's Ladder." Brian Preston, Saturday Night, April 1992.
- "Our Broken Relationship With The Society of Brothers." Samuel Kleinsasser, Concord Colony, MB, 1993.
- "Patent called 'root of all evil' " Terry Weber, Winnipeg Free Press, July 13, 1989.
- "Prairie Peace-makers." Doreen Mierau, The Saskatchewan Valley News, June 8, 1967.
- "Scapegoating the Hutterites." Fay Orr and Stephen Weatherbe, Alberta Report, 1984.
- "Stress and Conflict in an International Religious Movement: The Case of the Bruderhof." Timothy Miller, CESNUR/INFORM/ISAR conference, London, March 1993.
- "The Bruderhof." by John McManus, Winnipeg Free Press, October 22, 1983.
- The KIT Newsletter, Peregrine Foundation, San Francisco, CA, 1989 – 1997.
- "The Dark Years of the Bruderhof: book review by Katie Funk Wiebe." Mennonite Weekly Review, Newton Kansas, June, 1994.
- "The Emotional Acculturation of Hutterite Defectors." by Caroline M. Hartse, Journal of Anthropological Research, vol. 50, 1994.
- "The Prairieleut: A Forgotten Hutterite People." by Rod Janzen, Communal Societies Association, 1994.
- "The Society of Brothers who call themselves Hutterites: Some Personal Concerns." John A. Hostetler. (Unpublished article.)
- "Tradition no obstacle at Hutterites' high-tech plant." Ritchie Gage, The Globe and Mail, Toronto, ON, Nov. 10, 1986.
- "Tri-System Hutterite Project," EOF Hi-Lites, Alberta Education, Edmonton, AB, December 1983.

Photograph Credits

- **BM** Barb Mathieu
- **CFWS** Reprinted with permission from *Princes, Potentates, and Plain People,* by Reuben Goertz, Center For Western Studies
- **CKOS** CKOS-CICC Television, Yorkton, Saskatchewan
- **CLA** City of Lethbridge Archives
- **CM** Catherine Masuk
- **EW** Edna Wurtz
- **HM** Hannah Maendel
- **HM/TW** Hannah Maendel, courtesy of Tony Waldner
- **HMCC** Reprinted with permission from *History of the Hutterite Mennonites,* Hutterite Mennonite Centennial Committee
- **JE/TW** Joseph Eaton, courtesy of Tony Waldner
- **JW/BHP** Jim Warner, courtesy of Black Hat Productions, Inc.
- **LA/TW** Lawrence Anderson photo collection, courtesy of Tony Waldner
- **LG** Leonard Gross
- **LB/WH** Lorena Bach, courtesy of Walter Hoover
- **LB/MHLA** Lorena Bach, from Mennonite Historical Library and Archives, Goshen, Indiana
- **MW** Mary Wipf
- **MHLA** Mennonite Historical Library and Archives, Goshen, Indiana
- **MLA** Mennonite Library and Archives, North Newton, Kansas
- **NM** Norma Marshall
- **RB** Rolf Brednich
- **SH** Samuel Hofer photo collection
- **TW** Tony Waldner photo collection
- **WL** Wiebe Lemstra

Glossary

Bruderhof: Place or Community of the Brethren. In Europe, the Hutterian communities were typically referred to as Bruderhofs (plural). In North America, they are called colonies. The Society of Brothers' communities in the eastern United States, however, are referred to as Bruderhofs.

Dariusleit: The Darius people. One of three groups of communal Hutterites who came from the Ukraine to South Dakota in the 1870s. The leader of this group was Darius Walter, hence the name "Dariusleit." Today, these people live in the Canadian provinces of Alberta, Saskatchewan, British Columbia (only one colony); and in the states of Montana and Washington in the U.S.A.

Gebet: Prayer service. Gebet always refers to the evening church service. The service includes a traditional sermon, singing, and prayer. Except for singing, the congregation does not contribute to the service. When there are two ministers, they take turns delivering the service. Gebet is typically held every day of the week. But during the harvest—or on days when the women are busy gardening, canning fruits and vegetables, or butchering livestock—a service may be skipped.

gesangbuch /gesangbücher: These are standard High German words for songbook or songbooks. In the Hutterish language, however, the word used is singbüchel. (See Hutterish.)

Geschichtbuch (singular) **/ Gschichtbüchel** (singular) **Gschichtbüchlen:** The Chronicle books.

gman /gemein: Community.

Gmanshofter/Gemeinshafter: Communal people; particularly the Hutterite people.

huchzeit or **hochzeit:** Wedding festivity.

hulba: Festivity, engagement party. This term is not in use among theLehrerleit. (See Stübela.)

Hutterish: The Hutterite language. The first oral language Hutterite children learn. Classed as High German rather than Low German, this language most closely resembles a dialect spoken in the province of Carinthia, in Austria. When transmigrant Lutherans, exiled from Austria in 1755, joined the few remaining Hutterites in Transylvania, there was a considerable change from Tyrolese to Carinthian ethnicity among the Hutterites, because the Carinthians outnumbered the old Hutterites, who until then, predominantly spoke a Tyrolese dialect. The Hutterish language has a sprinkling of words that reflect their stay in Slavic areas, in Transylvania (Romania), in the Ukraine, and in North America. Hutterites are increasingly adopting English words, usually modifying them slightly to fit their own language patterns. Examples: farm becomes form, pipe-wrench becomes paip-rench, and move becomes mufn. (See Shriftshproch.)

Lehr: Sermon or Teaching. Lehr always refers to morning church services on Sundays and on religious holidays. The service includes the following, in this order: singing, a sermon, the prayer, another sermon, closing remarks, then the final singing.

Lehrerleit: The Teacher's people. One of three groups of communal Hutterites who came from the Ukraine to South Dakota in the 1870s. Lehrer means "teacher." The leader of this group was Jakob Wipf, a teacher, hence the name "Teacher's people." The Lehrerleit live in Alberta, Saskatchewan, and Montana.

Leit: People or folk. This term is also used for Hutterites older than fourteen or fifteen. When a teenager reaches that age, he or she becomes a member of the Leit, and has adult privileges. Throughout this book I have used the Hutterish word rather than the standard High German word "Leut," which has been wrongly used by virtually every scholar or journalist who has ever written about the Hutterites. In conversation, Hutterites always use the Hutterish word, "Leit." Virtually everyone who doesn't speak German mispronounces Leut as "Loot," when the proper pronunciation is Loit, as in "oil." Leit, on the other hand, is pronounced as "light." Leit could also be written as "Lait," which would not be incorrect in Hutterish German. I have spelled it as I have because it fits better into an English text, especially considering how often the word comes up. I suspect that most people would pronounce Lait as "late." *Late for what?*

lied/lieder: Song/songs.

liederbuch/liederbücher / liederbüchel / liederbüchlen: Songbook/songbooks.

Prairieleit: The Prairieleit Hutterites. Descendants of Hutterites who chose not to live communally when they settled in North America. Instead, they settled as individual homesteaders. These people are also referred to as Hutters (particularly in South Dakota) and Hutterite Mennonites.

Schmiedeleit: The Blacksmith people. One of three groups of communal Hutterites who came from the Ukraine to South Dakota in the 1870s. The leader of this group was Michael Waldner, who was also a blacksmith. Schmied means blacksmith, hence the name "Schmiedeleit." Today, these people live in Manitoba, North Dakota, South Dakota, and Minnesota.

Shriftshproch/Shriftshprache: The language of the Bible. All the Hutterites' traditional sermons are written in an antiquated German, referred to as "die Schriftshproch," as it was spoken in the 16th and 17th centuries.

stübela: A shivaree, festivity, or engagement party. This term is in use primarily among the Lehrerleit.

urnung: Order, community order, and church regulations.

vorsteher: Senior elder or bishop.

weggelufene: Weggelufene (plural), weggelufener (singular), weggelufen (adverb), weglaufen (verb). The literal meaning of the word is "runaway," but it is used for all people who leave the Hutterite lifestyle, even though they may not physically "run away." For simplicity sake, throughout this book I use the standard High German word for runaway. The actual word in Hutterish (also a form of High German) is wecchg'lufne, which I think doesn't read well on the page.

About the Author

Samuel Hofer grew up in a Hutterite community in southern Saskatchewan. He left Hutterite communal life in 1983. Since then, he has written and published several books, including *Born Hutterite* (a collection of stories) and *Dance like a Poor Man* (a novel). He is living near Saskatoon, Saskatchewan.